STAY PUT

Discover the power of consistency

Trey Jones

STAY PUT

Discover the power of consistency

Trey Jones

BLAZE
PUBLISHING

STAY PUT: Discover the Power of Consistency
Trey Jones

Published by Blaze Publishing House
www.blazepublishinghouse.com
P.O. Box 184
Mansfield, TX 76063
817.791.4388

This book or parts thereof may not be reproduced in part or in whole, in any form, stored in a retrieval system, or transmitted in any form by any means—electronic, mechanical, photocopy, recording, or otherwise—without prior written permission of the publisher, except as provided by United States of America copyright law.

Unless otherwise indicated, all Scripture quotations in this volume are taken from the *King James Version* of the Bible.

Scripture quotations marked NIV are taken from the *Holy Bible, New International Version*, copyright © 1973, 1978, 1984 by International Bible Society. Use by permission of Zondervan. All rights reserved.

Scripture quotations marked AMP are taken from the *Amplified Bible*. Old Testament copyright © 1965, 1987 by Zondervan Corporation, Grand Rapids, Michigan. New Testament copyright © 1958, 1987 by Lockman Foundation, La Habra, California.

Scripture quotations marked NKJV are taken from the Holy Bible, *New King James Version*, Copyright © 1982 by Thomas Nelson, Inc. Used by permission. All rights reserved.

Direct quotations from the Bible appear in italic type.

Manuscript Development by Kent Booth
Editing and interior design by Laura-Lee Booth
Cover design by Bobby McCullough

Copyright © 2010 by Trey Jones
All rights reserved.

Library of Congress Control Number: 2010908313

ISBN-10: 0982528922

ISBN-13: 978-0-9825289-2-1

Hope and I would like to dedicate this book to the honor and memory of our heroes, who are the most inspiring and consistent people we know, our grandparents. We truly realize that we are standing on the shoulders of giants who focused their lives in Christ while overcoming obstacles and challenges through their faith and integrity.

A.Z. and Mary Sharpe
C.R. and Kathleen Jones
E.L. and Millie Shirey
Guy "Buck" and Elizabeth Reed

ACKNOWLEDGMENTS

To the people of Life Center Church, thank you for your consistent dedication to the assignment God has placed on all of our lives.

I would like to thank the people who have believed in Hope and me through the years and have been consistent sources of encouragement, strength, accountability, and laughter—you know who you are! Life is better because we get to live it with all of you!

I would also like to thank the people at Blaze Publishing House for your help with this project.

CONTENTS

INTRODUCTION ... 11

1. LIFE ON THE MERRY-GO-ROUND ... 17
   Consistently Inconsistent

2. WATCH OUT! ... 33
   The Enemies of Consistency

3. DRY TIME AND DRIED UP ... 51
   The Results of Inconsistency

4. THE TALE OF TWO LADIES ... 67
   Consistency Brings Relationships

5. WORDS NOT REQUIRED ... 79
   Consistency Speaks

6. A GOOD NAME AND SO MUCH MORE ... 99
   Consistency Brings Reputation and Favor

7. DON'T JUST STAND THERE AND STARE ... 121
   Consistency Makes a Way

8. BEHIND CLOSED DOORS   135
   Consistency Brings Intimacy

9. THE KINSMAN REDEEMER   149
   Consistency's Ultimate Promise

10. ALL THE WORLD'S A STAGE   163
    Fruit of a Consistent Life

ENDNOTES   181

INTRODUCTION

If you've ever watched the television phenom, *American Idol®*, you've probably heard Simon Cowell—the judge we all loved to hate—comment to individuals on the consistency of their performances. While some contestants raise the roof with one performance and crash and burn the next, others have a string of good, solid performances week after week. They are a rare breed of contestant. Every week, they show the world how to survive under incredible pressure and adapt to extreme circumstances. They get little-to-no-sleep, learn new music at an incredible pace, and combat the nerves of performing in front of 30 plus million people each week—not to mention the judges who scrutinize their every move! What's the key element that causes these contestants to rise to the forefront as a finalist and the possibility of becoming the next "American Idol"?

Consistency.

It's the necessary ingredient for any individual desiring any level of success in life—in the business world, workplace, corporate world, church world, and in one's family life, marriage, and relationships. Study successful people and, even though they have not been perfect, one thing you will find in common with all of them is that they are consistent and never give up.

Although many of the things we will be discussing in this book are written to deal with modern-day situations, there is no better example which exemplifies consistency and the rewards it yields than the Biblical story of Ruth. Her life is one of not only tragedy, but also of restoration by a lifestyle of faithful consistency, diligence, and hard work. In the end, the fruits of her commitments pay off in huge proportions.

Now, if you are of the male gender and have picked up this book and begin to think, *"This book is about a woman? It must be a chick-book,"* you'd better stop and think again! There are several things to consider when using Biblical examples to translate into everyday life. For example:

- **THE WORD OF GOD IS NOT PARTIAL.** That's right. God's Word is not partial or gender-biased. If a story from the Bible happens to be about a woman, it will work for a man, as well and vice versa. Secondly, God's Word is not racially-biased. Skin color or ethnicity is of no relevance. Thirdly, whether you are a successful businessman or businesswoman, a full-time student, a housewife (a.k.a. "domestic engineer"), or the "average Joe," God's Word, diligently applied to your life, will work for you.

- **THE WORD OF GOD IS NOT GEOGRAPHICALLY BOUND OR LIMITED.** There's a well-known phrase in real estate that says, "Location, location, location!" Meaning, your success depends on your location and the location of your property. This might be true when selling a home or a business location; however, it is quite the contrary when dealing with God's Word. The principles found in the Bible will work no matter where you are located. There are no geographical boundaries which make it valid—or successful—in one place and ineffective in another. Whether you are reading this in Florida or the Philippines, God's Word knows no cultural boundaries.

- **THE WORD OF GOD IS TIMELESS.** Although events occurring in the Bible took place thousands of years ago, the spiritual truths and principles taught within those stories are still relevant today.

- **THE WORD OF GOD CONTAINS TYPES AND SHADOWS.** When we read the Bible, particularly the Old Testament which contains the story of Ruth, we have to understand the usage of types and shadows. This simply means that although the physical events which took place are thousands of years old, we are still able to draw from them spiritual principles and applications for daily living.

- **EVERYTHING IN THE OLD TESTAMENT IS A PHYSICAL PICTURE OF A NEW TESTAMENT SPIRITUAL REALITY.** If you grew up in church or went to vacation Bible school every summer as a child, you have probably heard a lot of Bible stories. Noah and the ark, Jonah and the whale, Daniel in the lion's den, or David and Goliath are just a few of the larger-than-life Bible stories that immediately come to mind.

Before Jesus' death, burial, and resurrection, God revealed Himself in the lives of His people with outward and physical manifestations. For that reason, a great portion of the Old Testament is made up of stories and accounts of these actual experiences. The same is true with the story of Ruth.

- **MANY TIMES, NAMES MEAN SOMETHING.** Many times, the names of locations or people, especially in the Old Testament, carry great significance and meaning. Discovering what these names mean will reveal powerful insights to what God is trying to reveal to us. Understanding the names in this story of the life of Ruth will greatly help you to fully understand God's intent and guidelines for achieving success and fulfillment.

Let me encourage you to start your new life of consistency by actually *finishing this book*! I don't say that as a weak, manipulative way to build my ego, but I truly believe a consistent life has to begin *somewhere* with *something* that is readily obtainable. So, take a chapter and day and, in just a little more than a week, you'll be finished and begin a new, disciplined life. There is nothing like the feeling of actually completing a task or goal. It's wonderful!

If you are ready to start living in control of your life and obtain the goals and purposes God has set before you, then let's dive in to this powerful story of faithfulness, consistency, and redemption... together.

Are you ready?

Start right now by preparing your heart with this simple prayer:

Father, thank you for my life. Thank you for every plan and purpose you have ordained for me. Open the eyes of my heart as I read this book and let Your truth about consistency and it's transformational power get down deep in my life. I do not want to live life going around the same mountains of frustration, failure, disappointment, and regret. I'm ready for change, and I need the help of the Holy Spirit to guide me through every adjustment. I am depending on you because you are the only true consistent One. I thank You that You want this for me, even more than I want it for myself. Thank You in advance.

In Jesus' name,

Amen

"There is nothing constant in this world but inconsistency."

Chapter 1

LIFE ON THE MERRY-GO-ROUND

Consistently Inconsistent

One day a year, millions of people set out to change their lives, turn over a new leaf, and become a better person by making their verbal declarations. It's called their New Year's resolutions. At the time, they're confident and bold, ready to conquer their personal demons of smoking, losing weight, dieting, exercising, becoming more organized, or being a better parent or spouse. The problem with these "resolutions" is that there is no "resolve" in them. Even though they sound good and carry good intentions, something is lacking.

Merriam-Webster's Dictionary lists one of the definitions for "resolution" as *"the act of determining; a firmness."*[1] The act of "determining" requires one thing: determination! This seems pretty elementary; and yet, it is the one area where most people fall short. Their flippant resolutions closely resemble throwing spaghetti on the wall just to see what sticks. It is one thing for someone to make a firm decision to change, but a completely different element to do whatever it takes to follow through and achieve their expected end. Because success in these areas requires determination, most people structure their lives around goals which require the least amount of effort, discipline, and brain power.

Every New Year, church leaders and pastors from around the globe throw out clichés which, at the moment, sound very inspiring and rally the troops.

Things like:

"You're going to breakthrough in 2002."

"2003 is the year to be free."

"There's more in 2004."

"Come alive in 2005."

"It's going to get fixed in 2006."

"2007 we're all going to Heaven!"

"Your life is great in 2008."

"Live divine in 2009."

There's nothing wrong with these sayings; however, by February 1, you begin to realize that just because it was proclaimed to be *"The year of the breakthrough,"* does not automatically make it come to pass. There must be a lifestyle of consistency to match the proclamation which, in turn, produces the desired results.

So, what happened to the promise of *"A new you in 2002,"* or *"Things are great in 2008"*? Very simply put, there are enemies which compromise our "resolutions" and reduce them to frustrations and downfalls. Some of them are painfully personal and hit home. The first step towards real progress and change is being completely honest and acknowledging the areas which have caused stagnation or worse, a backwards regression in life.

GOOD INTENTIONS GONE WAY BAD!

No one sets out a new resolution expecting to fail. However, no matter how good our intentions are, it doesn't take long for the "little foxes"[2] to spoil our goals. Philosopher William James, who lived during the mid-1800s and into the early 1900s, is quoted as saying:

> *"No matter how full a reservoir of maxims one may possess, and no matter how good one's sentiments may be, if one has not taken advantage of every concrete opportunity to act, one's character may retain entirely unaffected for the better. With mere good intentions, hell is proverbially paved."*[3]
>
> William James

Many of us start well; we start strong. The problem is, once the feeling of excitement over these new life-changes begins to wane—and it always does—so does the priority in which we devote to make it happen. It's inevitable, resolutions that are broken always leave a bad taste in our mouths. They reek of failure. More drastic cases can lead to depression, a lack of self-esteem, and feelings of inadequacy. In the end, we may never feel as though we can change for the better.

Let's take a look at some of the top resolutions for each New Year and the workings in which make them unobtainable.

> Resolution #1:
> *"I'm going to start going to the gym and lose weight."*

Can you guess which month has the highest amount of new gym enrollments? January! People are desperate to look good and feel good, but don't know how to get there on their own. But having a gym membership card in your wallet or purse is not the cure-all. There is much more involved in being successful.

One reason people fail at this lofty goal is the busyness of life. Schedules are complicated. Balancing work, family, and even maintaining a relationship with God can become quite the chore. Because of our fast-paced life, it's too easy to run by the local fast-food joint and pick up something to eat instead of enjoying a sit-down, healthy dinner at home. Why? Because that would mean we would have to plan ahead for meals—which is an enormous task for most. But, like with everything else, poor preparation and planning leads to poor progression.

So many people make the resolution to lose weight, but are always looking for the easy road! Like the magical diet pill which will eat away the pizza in your stomach before it is converted into pounds of unwanted fat. The truth is, there is no "wonder pill" or shortcut to achieve good health and a good figure or physique. It takes a firm decision, hard work, and self-discipline.

> **Resolution #2:**
>
> *"I'm going to spend more time with my family."*

Here is an all-too-familiar scenario:

The phone rings.

"Honey, I'm going to be a little late tonight coming home."

"Again? You were late yesterday, too."

"I just have things that I have to get done."

"But, you promised little Ricky you'd throw a few passes with him tonight. He has that big game this weekend, you know."

"I know, but I've gotta do what I have to do. We have bills, you know. It's not free having the lifestyle you enjoy so much. I'll be home later."

Click.

The phone hangs up.

The wife is either disappointed or mad as a hornet. She's heard those same lines too many times to number. The problem with this scenario is there is *always* more work to be done. But, by the time the dad gets home, the window of opportunity to do anything with his family has been lost. It's too late. Time to eat. Time for baths or showers. Time for bed. Time to wake up and do it all over again.

> Resolution #3:
>
> *"I'm going to get out of debt!"*

We are a *"live for the moment"* society and have the horrendous credit reports to prove it! For most people who have credit card debt and only pay the minimum balances, it will take 20 or 30 years to eliminate the balances owed. Think about it, you might be still paying for a dinner you ate 15 years ago! I sincerely applaud anyone who is trying to live debt-free. But if you desire this status, a consistent and very disciplined financial life isn't a suggestion—it's a requirement.

There is an old saying, which I love, that says:

"If your outgo is larger than your income, then your upkeep will be your downfall!"

Author Unknown

Of all the financial seminars and teaching tools that are available today, this statement stills proves to be some of the best advice on getting out of debt. Simply put—don't spend more than you make!

THE DEVIL ON THE NIGHTSTAND

Maybe you're one who loves to sleep and thinks your alarm clock is the devil incarnate. You've excused your way out of getting up early by saying, *"Well, I'm just not a morning person."* So, instead of getting out of bed and preparing for your day, you just hit that blessed snooze button. *"Ugh, just five more minutes! I just need five more minutes!"* Before you know it, five minutes quickly turns into 30. The results? Now, there is no time left to read your Bible or pray before getting to work. Going to the gym is out of the question, as well. So, you rationalize, *"Well, it's too late now. I'll just go tomorrow."* Unfortunately for most, that "tomorrow" never comes—not because they physically die, but because the priority dies in them.

TRUE CONFESSION

As I'm writing this book on consistency, I have a confession to make: I am dealing with an issue which is challenging my commitment level to the max! I know, most people think pastors live in a "perfect world" which is alienated from reality, but that is not the truth! And here is a perfect example.

> The first step towards real progress and change is being completely honest and acknowledging the areas which have caused stagnation or worse, a backwards regression in life.

Towards the end of 2007, a couple of guys from our church and I took a look at ourselves and realized our metabolism had gone on strike. Our six-pack abs were now more like washtubs! So, what was the natural course of action? To start a workout routine at our local gym, of course. We decided to dedicate three days a week to a workout schedule. Knowing that accountability comes with two or more people who are striving for the same goal, it seemed to be a great plan to keep us all motivated. More than just the obvious health reasons, we also wanted to be good examples to our kids and the people we lead. Everything was in place: the recognition of our current condition, the motivation to change, a plan of action, and—last but not least—accountability. We were ready and committed... then reality begin to raise its ugly head!

> Longevity...gives us the ability to see the big picture and work for lasting achievements.

Because of our varied and busy schedules, the only time we could all meet at the gym was 6 AM. (Ok, that's before the crack of dawn in Georgia, where we live, but we were committed and set our clocks accordingly.) I have to admit, the first seven months or so were fairly easy. During that time, I had nearly doubled my bench press and was feeling strong and energized. My motivation was so high, I would even go the gym in the afternoons, without the other guys, just to get in extra workout. It felt so good for people to say, "*Pastor Trey, your arms are getting bigger!*" My wife, Hope, was beginning to look at me in a way that I had not seen in a while—like I was her "hunk of burning love!"

The Christmas season arrived and began to demand later

and later hours for me at the church. This was okay because I am a self-proclaimed "night owl." But the demonic alarm kept going off at 5:30 AM, three days a week. I could feel the late nights taking their toll on me; and instead of making it to the gym three days a week, now it was two. Then two became one.

Inconsistency began to set in.

Finally one morning, I pulled myself out of the bed, put on my workout clothes and waltzed through the door of the gym at 6:05 AM. My workout partners began to applaud and one commented *(in a loving, concerned tone, of course)*, *"Hey, Pastor Trey, where have you been lately? Sleeping off all that chicken you've been eating?"* Needless to say, I was once again motivated to have this priority alive in me. Not just so the "chicken-eatin' preacher" jokes would end; but more importantly, that my life, in general, would be better.

WHEN THE GOING GETS TOUGH...

It never ceases to amaze me to watch professional athletes who make millions of dollars each year say after a bad game, *"We were just not motivated to play well tonight."* Not motivated? $35,000 a week is not enough motivation?

Obviously, money is not a defining factor in producing a consistent performance. However, there have been many blue-collar, middle-class workers who have retired and never missed a day of work. Some had never been late one day. Not one day late! Now *that* is a life of consistency which comes from the inside of person.

The question is usually not with our motives or intentions. We all want to change and live a better life. The real question is this: are we willing to be consistent enough to see a real difference? I have had people come to me with a great report of receiving the new job in which they have been praying and fasting for. A few months later I asked them, *"Hey, how's your new job going?"* *"Oh, Pastor Trey, you know, I quit and went back to my old place and took a huge pay cut."* *"Why?"* I would ask. *"Well, it was just too hard."* Is every job easy? No. Are there difficult times and situations? Yes. Being consistent, even in very difficult times and seasons is a major key to a successful life.

IN IT FOR THE LONG HAUL

Society as a whole has drastically changed over the years. My grandparents, for example, would not have left their house to go shopping without being dressed to the hilt. Today, people wear less clothes to the mall than my grandparents wore to bed!

Another extreme change has been the value of longevity. People, in general, do not plan for the long haul anymore. You probably do not have to be reminded that, in the United States, our divorce rate is over 50%.[4] Eighty percent of new businesses never last over five years.[5] In fact, most never make it past the two-year mark. What does this say? That longevity and consistency cannot be separated from each other.

Longevity is a amazing principle that holds many key characteristics to a consist life. In a nutshell, it is dedication and commitment personified. And there are great benefits to living a life dedicated to the long haul. Here are just a few:

- **LONGEVITY IS THE KEY TO A CHANGED LIFE.** This is so true. However, the benefits are not attained quickly. To stay with a potentially life-changing commitment for a matter of a couple of months does not produce many results. Life changes are ones which not only affect us individually, but also influence our future generations. Positive changes which occur in our lives over an extended period of time will become the platform for our children and grandchildren to excel from. Those platforms are built through our longevity and stick-to-it-ness.

- **LONGEVITY BRINGS CREDIBILITY.** When Hope and I first arrived in Macon to plant our church, no one really cared we were there. After the first year, a few people begin to show interest. Now, more than nine years later, we are reaching an entire community because credibility has been built through longevity. We are taken more seriously now, than we were in 1999. Don't get me wrong, those first few, long, and lean years were very trying. Discouragement was rampant. We constantly wrestled with the thought of, *"Did we make the biggest mistake of our lives?"* especially concerning our young children. Now, we can see this is exactly God's plan for our lives in this season. Longevity is paying off!

- **LONGEVITY BRINGS A SENSE OF ACCOMPLISHMENT.** It is hard to have very many accomplishments if our lives are a series of starts and stops. One of my greatest fears is to think one day I will look back and take inventory of

> One of the benchmarks of accomplishment is when your life adds value to the world around you.

my life and not like what I see. Actually, it is one of my greatest motivators, as well. You see, God's desire is to accomplish great things through all of us. These specific assignments are not just for us; they are to impact others, too.

One of the benchmarks of accomplishment is when your life adds value to the world around you. But this type of real success is not feasible without a working understanding of longevity. Longevity keeps us from just wasting our lives on menial tasks and gives us the ability to see the big picture and work for lasting achievements.

Ask yourself:

"What am I consistently giving myself to that will leave my city better for the next generation?"

"What family besides mine is better because I have committed to something bigger than me and followed through?"

History tells us time and again that the people who made the biggest impacts on their world were those who did not make excuses for their lack of staying power. They never used the common excuses like: "It's just not in my personality" or "I'm the type of person who starts things but never finishes." No, they stuck to it. They defied all odds and overcame whatever "personality quirks" they needed to conquer. In the end, they accomplished something great through their longevity. Today's world needs more people with this type of determination!

- **LONGEVITY INCREASES OUR LIVES.** Have you ever stopped to realize that your life will outlive you? What a great thought to know we are creating a legacy for future generations. It happened with King David in the Bible. He conquered all of the enemies who rose up against the people of God and established a value for God's presence among the people. But that wasn't David's ultimate goal; there was more he wanted to accomplish. His heart's desire was to build God a temple, but God would not allow him to do so because he was a man of war and bloodshed. So what did David do? Sit on his hands and pout? Throw away his dream and sink

> Longevity, especially in the midst of difficulty, will build confidence, establish credibility and earn the respect of others while setting up our kids and grandkids for greatness.

into depression? No! He saw something that would reach beyond his lifespan, and he prepared his son, Solomon, to fulfill the mission.

David understood the power of longevity and faithfulness to the purposes of God for his life, even if his son had to carry out the final accomplishment. In the end, Solomon built the Temple, and David's legacy was outliving his own life!

Longevity, especially in the midst of difficulty, will build confidence, establish credibility and earn the respect of others while setting up our kids and grandkids for greatness. How much more motivation do we need?

AS YOU BEGIN

At the outset of this book, let me encourage you to begin to examine your own life. Don't be afraid to ask yourself some questions like:

"Am I a sprinter who constantly needs breaks, or am I a distance runner who is committed to the long-haul?"

"Is my life a series of stops and starts with broken momentum?"

"Do I constantly make excuses for the inconsistencies in my life?"

"Can I take myself seriously, or do I constantly disappoint myself and see little credibility within?"

"Do I want to accomplish something great and have my life count? What legacy do I want to leave?"

Whether you are embarrassed by this self-assessment or actually feeling pretty good about it, there is always room for improvement. You have more to accomplish: more credibility to establish, more influence to gain, more transformation to experience, more lives to impact, more accomplishments to realize, and a legacy to build. The whole purpose of this book is to show how to break the bad cycles of inconsistency and discover the power and freedom of a consistent life.

Enjoy your journey!

"A man's doubts and fears are his worst enemies."

– William Wrigley

Chapter 2

WATCH OUT!

The Enemies of Consistency

The Body of Christ is at a place where God is doing tremendous things in our lives. At the same time, it is very easy to step back a little, take some time off, and lose our focus. For example, in the very height of God's blessings, people can become distracted and say, *"I don't have to be in the Word as much anymore,"* or, *"Why do I have to go to church every week?"* Isn't it funny that when all hell was breaking loose, those same people were at church for every service, answered every prayer call, and lifted their hands and voice in worship? All because they needed answers. They needed God to rain in their garden. And God demonstrated His faithfulness by bringing a spiritual rain which produced refreshing and renewal.

When someone's life is brought into order on the inside, then their external circumstances begin to change. Life is better with this new sense of positive momentum. They find themselves at a great new place emotionally and spiritually. But, herein lies the problem: most people are only used to *visiting* great new places and never *stay* any length of time. Take, for example, Disney World®. Millions of people from all over the world visit there each year. But, have you noticed that no one ever moves into the Magic Kingdom®? Spiritually speaking, it is the same way. How many people love to visit the better "place" God has brought them to, but never commit to live there? In a very short time, the momentum begins to normalize, and the emotional "buzz" wears off.

Missing one week of church turns into two. Two turns into four. Then two months have passed without any fellowship in the house of God, and they begin to wonder:

"Why am I so dry?"

"Why do I feel so cut off?"

"Where is God's presence in my life?"

The answers are simple. Somewhere down the line, one of the enemies of consistency has attacked...and won!

What are those enemies? Let's take a look at four of the most common ones that wage war against a life of consistency.

ENEMY # 1

Fatigue

Have you ever been tired? I mean *really* exhausted? Sure you have. We all have. Maybe you were on the road to your destiny, and life was good. God was the center of your focus. Your relationships were at their best, and you could almost put your life on cruise control. Then, something happened. The energy to serve God and the love for His Word began to dissipate. Your focus became distracted. The things which were once vital began to lose their importance. All of a sudden, you felt as if you were spiritually running out of gas. Then, up ahead on the road of life...you saw a rest area! Time to check out for a little while and take a break! Right?

Wrong!

There are no rest areas on the road to your destiny. There are exits, but even those can present a challenge in returning back on your path. Billboards on the highway always say, "Easy on, easy off." But just what constitutes "easy"? On your walk with God, there are so many temptations to exit—to check out for a little while—and then pick up where you left off. "Easy on, easy off." But, it is never that easy!

The enemy of fatigue is described this way in the Bible:

"And we desire that each one of you show the same diligence to the full assurance of hope until the end, that you do not become sluggish..."

Hebrews 6:11-12a

God's desire is plain: for us to be diligent—consistently working—in pursuit of the things which we are hoping for all the way to the end without becoming sluggish, lethargic, or fatigued. But these enemies are real and ones we must face. They are packaged in various shapes and forms—physical, mental, spiritual, and emotional.

Physical fatigue is real, but I believe the greatest enemy to forward progress is mental fatigue. Mental fatigue can crater our motivation, inspiration, desire, and creativity. It can feel like we have put our internal gearshift into neutral and are stuck going nowhere, fast! Most people interchange this type of mental slothfulness with laziness, but this is not always the case. Being sluggish in our mind is actually more related to monotony than laziness. Momentum is replaced with fatigue; genuine zeal digresses into disinterest with a take-it-or-leave-it attitude.

For Believers who have a high work ethic, this type of attack can produce an enormous amount of discouragement. And here is what they usually come to realize: they are trying to accomplish everything within their own strength! Usually, a bout with mental fatigue moves them to the place of understanding just how vital it is to rely on the power of Holy Spirit to work through them!

As a pastor of a local church, I have seen people start working in a particular area of ministry with enough vitality to make the Energizer Bunny™ look like he was in a coma. Full of vision, drive, stamina, and determination, they begin to serve tirelessly in the ministry God had called them to. Then one day, they come to the stark realization that the words "ministry" and "work" are synonymous! *"Pastor Trey, let's get 'er done"* becomes replaced with *"I didn't know this was going to be so hard. Can I have three months off to rest?"*

Please understand; resting is okay. Everybody needs to go on a vacation and take their family to a different, refreshing environment. But, here's the catch: let God go on vacation with you! Invite the Lord to hang out by the pool in Florida or ski the mountains of

Colorado with you. Rest is good, just as long as you are not resting *from* God.

One of the greatest sources of fatigue is taking on more responsibility than is humanly possible to manage. Some people just want to serve...in every ministry at the church! Every night gets taken up with a meeting here, an outreach there, and something else over there. Their ambition and heart is to please God and His people, but they over commit. Before long, their motivation is replaced by exhaustion, and they quickly become disheartened.

The best way to avoid the enemy of fatigue is to ask the Lord what *His* plans for you are. Then, stay the course. Prepare to serve for the long-haul. This is when you are the most effective for the Kingdom of God.

> **ENEMY # 2**
>
> Impatience

"Lord I want patience,...and I want it NOW!" Maybe you have never prayed this prayer, but I can practically guarantee that you have thought it, or know someone who has. It is part of our human nature!

Impatience is an enemy that is almost always self-inflicted. People will start with ambition; but when their desired results are not almost instantaneous, they grow impatient and quit. We are plagued with the need for instant gratification. Take adults who

STAY PUT

enroll back into college. They convince themselves, *"Two years and I will have my degree! That will practically seem like overnight!"*

Wrong!

About half-way through the first year, the reality of routine begins to sink in. *Sports Center*™ and *Access Hollywood*™ are now replaced by projects and reports! While the frustration builds, they begin to ask themselves, *"Is this thing ever going to end?"* Sadly, many cave into the pressure of inconsistency and never obtain their goal. The enemy of impatience wins.

> There are no rest areas on the road to your destiny.

Not only do unrealistic expectations give way to impatience, so do the disappointments with past failures. Just when a new opportunity presents itself, we are quickly reminded of the last three times we tried and subsequently fail. This releases a sense of reproach, robbing us of the consistency needed to succeed in this new endeavor. However, maybe this will be the time to break the chain and pattern of failure and begin a new life of victory and fulfillment!

Over the years, Hope and I have had a few occasions where we were almost derailed because of disappointments. They primarily came in two ways: (1.) other people, and (2.) not seeing our dream manifest fast enough. When we moved to Macon, GA in 1999, we came with two small children in diapers and little-to-no money, *but* had a great dream and a desire to see God do something unique and powerful in our community. Our motivation was high, and we were ready for the task at hand...or so we thought.

We had only met two people in Georgia before we moved, so our first few months were lean—very lean. Then, a few people started to attend the church, and we could see increase. We were so sure God was sending us the "foundational" people every church needs to build upon. But, but by the fifth month, we were awakened to a dose of reality. Two of our "foundational" people bolted; and another couple, in whom we had invested huge amounts of time, jumped ship with a lame excuse! I was very tempted to throw my hands up and say, *"God, what's up with this? The very people you put here to us help just rejected us and walked out the door!"* It was tough, and we were ready to pack up and leave. The enemy of impatience, through disappointment, was at work—full-throttle! But, we continued on.

A few years later, despite meeting in an un-air-conditioned, rented school gymnasium, the church grew. (If you've ever been to Georgia in the summer, you know air conditioning is right next to godliness!) Momentum was building. We were adding staff to accommodate for the growth. Everything was going according to plan!

And then, it started.

First, one of our staff members decided he needed to move. Soon after, certain individuals began to unjustifiably slander our youth pastor. Their poison of lies and half-truths spread through our congregation. Eventually, they set up meetings with people from the church dubiously portrayed as *"we just needed someone to talk to."*

Trying to understand their position (which I never did), I would graciously sit in these meetings. Very quickly, it became obvious that we had some serious rebellion issue, which in the end resulted in about 30% of the congregation walking out the door. Honestly, this was one of the darkest times of my life.

Not only were Hope and I very hurt by the people we loved, but we also had an internal sickening from watching our dream drag on and on. Actually, at this point, we really felt as if we were going backwards. I never will forget our 30-minute conversation about quitting. We were tired and had grown very impatient with people and with God. But two things would not let us quit: the commitment we had made to our youth pastor and his family and our children. Circumstantial pressure was not going to make us break our covenant to either one of these! We came to the realization that if we were to quit now, what message would it send to our children? How could we ever expect them to keep going through tough times? In our minds, the 30% of the congregation could go, but we were determined not to allow anyone to steal our children's platform.

The last part of Hebrews 6:12 says, *"...but imitate those who through faith and patience inherit the promise."* We are then reminded of Abraham who *"patiently endured"* until he obtained the promise. How many times did he and Sarah try to conceive before they produced a child? But they endured. Before David ever became an Israelite hero, he was a no-name shepherd boy who was overlooked by his own father. Moses spent 40 years in the desert, running from God, before he was a leader to be heralded throughout the ages.

John Maxwell, who has been a tremendous voice concerning the principles of leadership for many years, was touted as a modern, "overnight success." Little did anyone know, he had been the senior pastor of a growing church in California for over 20 years before he ever obtained national recognition. Once, while addressing a congregation of leaders, he said, *"I'm an overnight success that has been 20 years in the making!"* Remember this: nothing great comes overnight; there are no overnight successes.

Never allow impatience to cause you to quit on your dream. There is a candid greatness and power when you simply continue to show up. God honors persistency and patience—which is a fruit, or characteristic, of the Holy Spirit. Patience is not a trait which God brings upon you like Spiderman's web. Instead, He develops it deep within your heart until your character reflects His character. Don't run from the classroom, nor allow impatience to rob you or your family of the platform for lasting change.

Endure to the end!

Enemy # 3

Distraction

This section is very easy for me to write because I am one of the most easily-distracted people you will ever meet...hang on...

The phone's ringing...

Wait, I just received an email...

Now my cell phone is going off...

...Ok, I'm back!

It does not take much to get my head to spin and my focus off track. I would have been the A.D.D. poster child—that is, if we would have even known it existed back in the day. Growing up as an only child, I sometimes now use my adulthood to make up for my alone time as a kid. I am very extroverted, like to live out loud, and love to have other people around. (Yes, I talk to myself, but I do *not* answer myself...at least, not always!) Sad to say, I have allowed distractions to rob me of my focus and consistency more than once.

One thing I have learned: distractions come in all shapes and sizes and range from the very silly to the very significant. A silly distraction would be allowing a hobby or interest to take too much of your time and thus make you ineffective. A significant distraction would be someone in your family receives a bad report from their doctor.

Silly distractions are usually self-induced and are things you can take control over. When you allow your self-discipline to slip, it generally results in your priorities becoming out of whack, which buries you in a pit of inconsistency and unproductiveness. Significant distractions, on the other hand, are things which are out of your control. Given the opportunity, you would not allow them in your life because they threaten so much more than just your time and focus. They are issues that will dramatically change your life.

In Galatians 5:7, Paul asked the church in Galatia, "You were running a good race. Who cut in on you?"

Paul was writing this to the early church who had started out well and was making progress. But, somewhere down the road, they stepped off course and became distracted! In their case, distractions came in the form of false teachers and wrong information. Someone from the outside came in and got them off course. But let's be honest, that's usually not the case with us!

> Our greatest deterrent is usually... *ourselves!*

Our greatest deterrent is usually...*ourselves!*

I admit: no one can get me off course like I can! Usually it is because I said, *"Yes!"* to something I do not need, or said, *"No!"* to something I do need. As a pastor, I believe the highest priorities in my life must be prayer and study. But, it is amazing how those two simple commitments are always challenged by interruptions—the vast majority being self-induced.

While we might be our own worst enemy, we are not completely isolated from others who can divert us from accomplishing our priorities and goals. (And no, I am not referring to our spouse and children!) What about the negative people who always seem to surface at the most inopportune time? We have all had them.

These people remind me of a bucket of crabs. Just as one crab tries to crawl out and move on to greater things, another one reaches up and pulls him back. What a perfect picture of how people try to keep you locked into their "bucket" of mediocrity. The truth is, they don't want to see you succeed! Why? Because, your success will put a higher demand on their life. Negativity and guilt trips are their chief ammunition and conversations are their weapons to paralyze you from moving forward to higher achievements.

...our world needs people who know who they are and do not deviate from their identity.

Beware of the crabs in your life!

The jealous co-worker, who sees the writing on the wall that one day you are going to be his boss, will try to curb your enthusiasm and work ethic by saying, *"Why don't you stop kissing up to the V.P. of the department? You know that won't get you anywhere."* What about the lazy friend who has no ambitions or dreams of their own? You've made the commitment not to be distracted and to focus your energies and time on the dream God has given you. Then the guilt trip begins. *"I see how it is! You just don't have time for me anymore."* Then, there is always the beloved family member (God bless 'em) who wants you to live in their misery and never advance. You go off to college, obtain your degree, and start a career...only to be greeted with, *"So, you think you're better than us now, don't you?"*

Distractions, whether self-induced or external, can steal, kill, and destroy the consistency required to fulfill your purpose and dream. Take a lesson from Nehemiah and the people of Jerusalem.

While working diligently to rebuild the walls of the city, they were faced with countless enemies who tried to discourage and distract them from completing their mission. They worked with one hand on the wall and kept a sword in the other. Obviously, I am not insinuating you should physically use the sword on the people who are keeping you from your goal! However, you should refuse to give in to their insecurities and lack of vision. Set boundaries to defend the priorities of your life.

Believe me, if *you* don't protect them, no one else will!

> Enemy # 4
>
> Fear

Of all the enemies of a consistent, productive life, fear seems to be most rampant. We all know people who are afraid of everything. Their entire life is summed up by questions like, *"What if...?"* or statements like, *"I just don't know!"* We live in a world that has become paralyzed by fear, mainly being afraid of the unknown. Not knowing what the next step looks like, people choose to not move forward at all. They usually do not make any advancement until they find reassurance from someone else who has "done it" or "been there." Even then, they are always talking about what they want to do; but fear renders their actions inconsistent. You've seen the kid who tells everyone how he is going to jump off of the high dive. He walks to the end of the board 10 times and watches 132 other kids jump off first, just to make sure it will not hurt...and is still very cautious. His aspirations do not match his performance because of one, overriding factor:

Fear.

During our relocation to Georgia, Hope and I were very unsure of who we were. Our biggest ambition was for this church to succeed and be an encouragement to the people in our region. In order to accomplish this task, we needed people. Knowing that most people are not typically drawn to those they do not like, our first mission was to get people to like us. As simple as this sounded on the onset, it proved to be more than we bargained for. For the first year, our plan was progressing fairly well. I intentionally did not preach any messages which would be considered challenging or threatening. Over the course of my life, I had ministered many times and had seen great results, but this time was different. There seemed to be so much more at stake. The bottom line was, I was afraid of failure.

> Fear is rooted in the love of self. Because we love ourselves so much, we are afraid of getting hurt, disappointed, rejected, or misunderstood.

After our first year, I soon realized our plan was not working. My fear of failure was completely changing the way I ministered and caused me to be very inconsistent in my decisions and leadership style. Honestly, I felt like a fraud; and there was no consistent momentum in the church. The passion to really teach the Word of God was burning on the inside of me; however, what was coming out of my mouth was not consistent with my convictions. This struggle of really defining who I was began to take its toll.

It was about this time when God began to put people into our lives who became a powerful voice and influence. They began to help us shape our destiny and, more importantly, recognize who we *really* were. Suddenly, I began to see how our community needed me to be consistent with who God created me to be, instead of the person I thought they would accept. Our church began to grow, even though I found out some people did not like me! (Oh, well.) My passion to see people changed quickly began to override my deep, insecure need for approval. I started to realize that it was none of my business what other people thought about me.

This was my true freedom!

Fear is rooted in the love of self. Because we love ourselves so much, we are afraid of getting hurt, disappointed, rejected, or misunderstood. We live with the fear of failure. To avoid these painful experiences, we just go along to get along, instead of pursuing God's destiny for us and staying consistent—even in stormy times.

It grieves me to watch young people who are always trying on different personalities and personal images, all for the sake of social acceptance. Then, when I am around their parents, I see how they are caught in the exact same trap—only 25 years older! Insecurity and fear has reproduced insecurity and fear.

Fear will keep you inconsistent. Now, more than ever, our

> God did not create us to be chameleons—constantly changing to adapt to our surroundings—and be controlled by insecurities and inferiority issues.

world needs people who know who they are and do not deviate from their identity. The Bible says, *"For God has not given us a spirit of fear, but of power* (to overcome anything) *and of love* (love for Him and what He loves) *and of a sound mind* (safe, guarded, God-inspired thoughts)" (2 Timothy 1:7, parenthetical comments added). We cannot compromise our values and integrity just to please people. God did not create us to be chameleons—constantly changing to adapt to our surroundings—and be controlled by insecurities and inferiority issues. Rather, we strive to walk with a deep sense of purpose, identity, and security which produces consistent relationships, decisions, productivity, and progress. When we live this type of life, we demonstrate the masterpiece God originally designed for us to live.

LIVING CONSISTENTLY

By now, you have probably figured out that having consistency to your life is not easy! If it was, then everyone would live that way. But hang in there, the rewards of a long, fruitful life are incredible—not only for your life, but for your children and future generations, as well.

Nowhere else is this more beautifully portrayed than in the story of Ruth. It paints a beautiful backdrop of how a consistent life has the ability to overcome major obstacles, obtain unusual favor, and positively affect every area of life, while impacting the world. Don't be fooled, though. Her story begins on the rollercoaster of inconsistencies. But one thing is quickly established (and is still true today)...

...God is always consistent.

It is just His nature. He is the One who keeps His Word, who is faithful to the end, and whose mercy and goodness are abundant and never-ending. He is never double-minded or moody and does not deviate based on popular opinion or His emotional state. His ultimate desire is for us, as His children, to mirror His consistency for our lives and to influence the world around us.

No matter where you are in life right now, you can change. The story we are about to see is God's blueprint in developing a consistent, unwavering, and productive life.

Let the story begin!

"... inconsistency with ourselves is the greatest weakness of human nature."

– Joseph Addison

Chapter 3

DRY TIME AND DRIED UP

The Results of Inconsistency

> *"Now it came to pass in the days when the judges ruled, that there was a famine in the land. And a certain man of Bethlehemjudah went to sojourn in the country of Moab, he, and his wife, and his two sons. And the name of the man was Elimelech, and the name of his wife Naomi, and the name of his two sons Mahlon and Chilion, Ephrathites of Bethlehemjudah..."*
>
> Ruth 1:1-2

Famine and destruction. What a way to start a story about the power of consistency! But, it is a mirror of many people's lives today. It is also a very accurate view of the spiritual and social conditions of Israel at this time in history. Basically, the people of God lived on a spiritual rollercoaster. Individually and corporately—inconsistency was the norm. One moment, they are on a spiritual high, loving God. They begin to seek the Lord and walk in obedience. The nation begins to experience the life and blessing of consistently following God's commands. Then, the next thing you know, their faith begins to wane; and their focus on the Lord diminishes. They become distracted and tempted to align themselves with false gods, bringing them to places of unfaithfulness. When this happens, all hell breaks loose around them!

Sounds too familiar, doesn't it?

Israel's disobedience and inconsistencies removed them from under God's hand of protection. They were plundered and terrorized by their enemies, but soon realized the error of their ways. Consequently, Israel repents and comes back to God. And God—with His ever-constant faithfulness and mercy—answered their cry of repentance. He sent a leader, also called a judge, who helped deliver them from their oppressors. And just like that, Israel was back on the mountaintop!

> When we live a life of inconsistency, things begin to dry up and die.

People like Deborah, Gideon, and Samson became God's agents of restoration. But very quickly, Israel would *again* begin a swift decent downward. Rollercoaster up. Roller-coaster down. Yo-yo up. Yo-yo down!

It was during this time of instability and inconsistency that a famine came to the people of God. Not because God wanted to punish them, but rather it was a self-imposed judgment brought through disobedience. Things began to dry up and die. Where God's presence was once enjoyed, now there was no life and no tangible presence of God—all because of the rollercoaster ride.

The same scenario happens today!

When we live a life of inconsistency, things begin to dry up and die. The heat gets turned up, and there is little relief. Times of refreshing are few and far between. Life's situations become difficult, and we start to live in a spiritual famine. The ground becomes hard, so planting new seed is extra laborious and almost ridiculous. But then, why even plant new seed if you can't water it? Fruitfulness and productivity are nearly impossible during famines. No water, little seed, and hard soil resulted in death. It is an all-too-often occurrence with the Body of Christ today.

On the surface, our walk with God might feel good and seem right...until one day, we wake up and ask,

"Why is my marriage so dry?"

"Why is my relationship with my kids not working?"

"Why can't I feel anything in a worship service?"

It might not have anything to do with the musicians on the stage or the people who greeted us at the door. More than likely, we have grown inconsistent in some areas of life which is reflected by the dryness of our soul. Spiritual famine has set in. Our heart becomes hard. The seed of God's Word has a difficult time getting through. Productivity and fruitfulness declines, and we cannot get ahead. While God is raining blessings on those around us, we feel dry. Why? Is it God's fault? No. Is our pastor or spiritual leader to blame? Probably not. The truth is, it is very difficult for God to pour out blessing on an inconsistent garden!

THE BREAD OF LIFE

Now, it is not my mission to take you on a journey of Greek and Hebrew words and definitions. (It would probably defeat your commitment of being consistent and finishing this book!) However, certain names and places are extremely relevant in the Bible and provide tremendous insight.

For instance, Ruth chapter one, verse one, says that a man named Elimelech lived in Bethlehem-Judah. The word Bethlehem, which is also the place where Jesus was born, actually means *"house of bread."* (How interesting that the Bread of Life was born in the *"house of bread!"*) The Bible says right in the middle of Israel's famine and deprivation, God still provided bread, sustenance, strength, and nourishment—and He has never stopped!

In today's world, all of these provisions are found in God's Word, also known as the Bread of Life. Jesus knew the power of the Word when He responded to the temptation in the desert by saying, *"Man shall not live by bread* (natural bread) *alone, but by every word* (spiritual bread) *that proceeds* (presently spoken) *from the mouth of God"* (Matthew 4:4, parenthetical comments added). God's Word is the constant Bread of Life and is always available...no matter how dry our life may seem.

All we have to do is eat!

DON'T STARVE AT THE BUFFET

Growing up close to the coast of South Carolina, I always loved the all-you-can-eat seafood buffets. Many nights, my dad and I would spend hours in those restaurants, trying to eat our body weight in crab legs! He always told me, "Trey, we'll start with the other stuff like shrimp, fish, and anything that looks appetizing and then comes the serious part—those crab legs." We were serious crab leg eaters!

Before we indulged ourselves, we always made sure we had a plate for trash and another plate for the shellers, some melted butter, and about 50 pounds of napkins! Then, it was time to get to work. Of course, part of our mission was to always try to eat our money's worth—and those seafood buffets were not cheap! My dad and I always left satisfied, and I'm sure the restaurant owners were glad to see us go!

Those restaurants were usually full of people stuffing their faces just like us. But what if someone paid the same amount as we did, had full access to the same food, but only sat there and watched us eat? What a tragedy...for them! To enjoy the full benefits of the buffet, takes more than desire; it takes participation. They would have to get a plate, some silverware, and a lot of napkins; and then dive in!

Spiritually, it's the exact same way. God's buffet—better known as His Word—encompasses all of the spiritual nourishment we would ever need. Yet, Christians live in famine and dry places, while the very Bread of Life is so readily available. They starve while looking at the spiritual buffet right in front of them. The Word of God can jump off the page and come to life in everyone else around them, but if they do not participate, they starve.

The American church is probably the guiltiest. Familiarity of spending so much time *around* the Word causes us to believe we are actually spending time *in* the Word. This is a deception of the enemy. While we are surrounded by spiritual food, we sometimes do not allow the Bread of Life to actually get *in us*! Thus, we dry up.

BEST OF TWO WORLDS

Elimelech didn't just live in Bethlehem. There was another part to the region known as the Providence of Judah, and they worked together. The word "Judah" means "*praise*." Praise is what brings God's presence. Elimelech and his family lived in the best of two worlds! A place with "strong word" *and* "strong praise!" But yet, they lived in famine!

Sound familiar?

How many Christians today are in this very same situation? They are involved in a church with a strong word and a tangible presence of God, but they live in spiritual scarcity. They are starving at the spiritual buffet! It's obvious that just being around the Word and a great atmosphere of praise is not enough. There has to be participation. The Bible says we must taste and see that the Lord is good! (Psalms 34:8)

THE RIGHT MIX

Healthy churches today still have this combination—a strong word mixed with a strong atmosphere of God's presence. However, the scales can be tipped too heavy on one side or the other.

For example, many churches today are driven by the Word (which in itself is not bad), but they have no atmosphere or real expression of worship. Actually, worship is lumped in with the announcements and other "non-essential" items. They just want to get to the Word. This is not a good balance, as these models lean toward strict legalism and put no emphasis on the expressions of thanksgiving and praise.

> Spiritual dryness will cause you to make decisions that, in hindsight, seem totally crazy!

Then, there are those churches which are praise-driven but have very little emphasis on the teaching of God's Word. It's all about *"getting your praise on"* which, again, is not a bad thing in itself. But, the scales are tipped. This type of church generally produces an emotionally-charged atmosphere, but seriously lacks spiritual substance.

What does God desire? Bethlehem-Judah. The place where *both* His presence (praise) and His power (Word) are in operation together. We need to be encouraged and challenged by His Word *and* experience His presence through worship. If the scales are tipped too far either side, then we become argumentative legalists or hyped-up ignoramuses! The world we live in needs to see us—real Christians—as an expression of God's grace, and ones who know the power of His Word. It is possible. We can live in a present-day Bethlehem-Judah!

But even in the middle of the place God has ordained for you, spiritual dryness can take its toll! You can start to have thoughts like, *"I can't feel anything here anymore,"* or, *"This is not working for me. I need to look elsewhere."* These are signs of spiritual drought. Elimelech and his family were in the exact same place, and they made the mistake of a lifetime: they moved without God telling them to move! They left their place of destiny—their place of inheritance and generational blessing—without any specific direction. Their excuse sounds so familiar: *"I'm not getting fed here anymore."*

The real question is, "Why did they really leave everything God had ordained for them?" Obviously, it wasn't due to the lack of spiritual nourishment. They lived in the very place called the House of Bread! What was lacking—and is still lacking in the Body of Christ today—was the hunger for the Bread of Life, which is so easily accessible.

People are still starving at the buffet!

FROM THE BREAD HOUSE TO THE FREAK SHOW

As if it wasn't bad enough that Elimelech moved his family without God's blessing, the place they moved to was even worse. (Spiritual dryness will cause you to make decisions that, in hindsight, seem totally crazy!) Their new destination was a country just outside of Bethlehem called Moab. Interestingly enough, Moab was named after a man who was the son of Lot. The fact that he was Lot's son was not so significant; however, the *way* he became the son of Lot is very intriguing.

In Genesis Chapter 19, you find the story of Lot and his daughters. They had rebelled against God and, eventually, found themselves in a place of total isolation with no connection to any other people. Lot's daughters were very discouraged as they watched their opportunity for childbirth dissipate. Then, they devised a plan. After getting their father, Lot, drunk, they had sex with him in hopes to become pregnant. And it worked.

Lot's oldest daughter become pregnant and gave birth to a son, Moab, whose name is literally interpreted: "incest." Lot's second daughter thought, *"Hey, if it worked for my sister, it will work for me."* She also became pregnant and gave birth to Benammi. (And you thought Jerry Springer had some freaky guests?)

Later in years, Moab's people, better known as the Moabites, became the source of one of the greatest sinful falls to the Children of Israel. The Moabite women seduced the men of Israel into improper, sexual relations. In one occasion, this brought a plague upon God's people and 24,000 people died.

Benammi became the leader of the Ammonites. Their claim-to-fame was their worship practices of drunken orgies. The children who were conceived and later birthed during these worship services were then sacrificed to their god, Molech. (I believe we can all agree that Lot and his daughters gave a whole new meaning to the word "dysfunctional.")

Elimelech—which means *"my God is King"*—had all of God's promises of blessing. All they had to do was stay put. Stay consistent and faithful in the place God had placed him. It sounds pretty simple, right? But, one of the enemies of consistency—*impatience*—led Elimelech to leave the place of blessing. And the stakes were high! This one decision led his entire family into rebellion. No longer was God King. Now, Elimelech was calling the shots!

Little did he know the price it would ultimately cost him.

A COSTLY PIT STOP

"And they went to the country of Moab, and remained ."

Ruth 1:2b

Most all Bible scholars agree that Elimelech's journey to Moab was never intended to be enduring. They were only staying as guests in a lodge to "take a little break." Nothing permanent. In a little while, they would move back to their homeland and continue right where they left off. No harm, right? Then, the unthinkable happened:

"Then Elimelech, Naomi's husband, died; and she was left, and her two sons."

Ruth 1:3 (NKJV)

Can you imagine the perplexity that overcame Naomi and her sons? Surely, they began to ask themselves, *"What happened? All we were doing was taking a break. We weren't planning on staying here. This is just a temporary journey. How could this possibly happen?"* What started out to be just a "pit stop" ended up costing

Elimelech his very life. But, the sad reality is this: before Elimelech died physically, he had already begun to die, spiritually!

Today, this exact same thing happens to many, many Christians.

In the place where there is a strong presence of worship and solid teaching of God's Word, the atmosphere is filled with revelation. It is inevitable. In this type of setting, God's vision for our lives can be discovered. Vision produces life! Destiny is discovered and shaped! Dreams come to life, and we thrive in this atmosphere. But, the opposite is just as true.

Without vision—or the continual revelation of what God says about our life—we die. When we lose God's kingship over our lives, things begin to die. Dreams die. Relationships die. Vision dies. A feeling of self-worth and confidence dies. Motivation dies. And the list goes on and on.

Obviously, Elimelech started to die *before* he ever moved his family from Bethlehem-Judah. Right in the very middle of God's Word and God's presence, emotional and spiritual death began to take its toll. Fatigue began to change motivation into frustration. What seemed to be a harmless detour has now become a nightmare. And, it wasn't over!

> **"Now they (Naomi's sons) took wives of the women of Moab: the name of the one was Orpah, and the name of the other Ruth. And they dwelt there about ten years."**
>
> **Ruth 1:4 (NKJV)**

Ten years? This temporary trip has now stretched itself out into quite a chunk of time. Isn't it amazing how one, miniscule step back somehow turns into an extended stay? What started as a short trip has now become a permanent dwelling for Naomi and her family. Little did they know how this one decision would soon be the defining point of their entire lives.

THE POWER OF ONE DECISION

Ruth has been left with her two sons, Mahlon and Chilion. Interestingly enough (here we go again!), their names mean, "*sickly, diseased,*" and "*whiner.*" Get this picture: Naomi had it all—a great husband, two sons, living in the very place of revelation and praise—and with one decision, her life became a wreck. Now, she is without God's kingly rule in her life, which provided a sense of provision and protection. As well, she has a whiner and a sickly child to attend to *by herself*. And just when she thought it could not be any worse:

> **"Then both Maholon and Chilion also died; so the woman survived her two sons and her husband."**
>
> **Ruth 1:5**

Wow! The power of one, wrong decision! And those decisions affect more than just ourselves.

Naomi's boys were probably in their early adolescence when they decided to move. These boys were innocent, yet they eventually paid the same price as their father did because of *his* disobedience! Just as a life of consistency and longevity can be a platform of success for our children, the opposite is just as true. Our inconsistencies can produce painful experiences and provide great amounts of baggage for them to have to sort through. For Elimelech and Naomi, one decision became painfully costly.

The Bible gives many examples of how this principle is true. Take Abraham and Sarah, for instance. God gave Abraham the promise of a child, but Sarah was old and beyond childbirth age. So, what did Abraham do? He took matters into his hands and impregnated Sarah's handmaiden. She gave birth to Ishmael, but he was *not* God's chosen son for Abraham; and Ishmael rebelled. Today, thousands of years after the fact, nations from around the world are at the height of a "holy" war. Tens of thousands of innocent lives have been lost over the faction of "Who is the son of promise?" One decision to make God's promise come to pass with a natural solution has wreaked havoc for many, many generations.

On the other hand, Jesus was faced with one of the most crucial and life-altering decisions ever to face any human being in the Garden of Gethsemane. Facing the horrific agony of death by crucifixion, Jesus made a decision which would transcend many generations. With the weight of the entire world on his shoulders, Jesus uttered these words: *"O My Father, if it is possible, let this cup pass from Me; nevertheless, not as I will, but as You will"* (Matthew 26:39). Jesus was—and still is—the consummate example of consistency, even to His death on the cross. He knew His mission and stayed the course all the way to His death and resurrection.

The power of one decision!

Now, think about how decisions—good or bad—affect those

around you. For example, one decision to end a marriage has a wake of effects. Children, grandparents, other relatives, and friends will all feel the sting. The same is true when a marriage partner chooses to leave Bethlehem for seduction. Many things die. The ability to trust dies, along with a vision for longevity in a relationship. Intimacy dies. Confidence dies. And the list of spiritual and emotional demise goes on and on. In reality, children are left to clean up their parents' messes and pay the tab! If the messes aren't cleaned up, the rejection, betrayal, dysfunction, and bitterness are perpetuated throughout future generations. That's not the legacy we want to leave.

Now, please do not take me wrong. Over the years, I have seen God completely restore and repair many relationships which have been unraveled by inconsistency. Marriages which seemed hopeless, God has redeemed and brought hope and life. The Bible says that His mercies are new every morning (Lamentation 3:22-23), and His grace is sufficient for every situation (2 Corinthians 12:9). There is hope, and God is the ultimate redeemer of lost time and can restore fragmented situations. This is His nature!

In the same manner, one *good decision* can have unbelievable ramifications. Take, for instance, a family who has no Christian heritage, and then someone in the family receives salvation. One decision to follow Christ can change many generations to come! The same would be true of the person(s) who rise up and break years of curses and weaknesses. One decision to attend church regularly, tithe and offer, or renounce an addiction may pave the way for others to live in God's best. It's the power of one decision!

TAKE RESPONSIBLITY

A little bit later in this same chapter, Naomi falls into a snare which plagues our society: refusing to take responsibility for actions and decisions. Verse 13 says:

> *"...for it grieves me very much for your sakes that the hand of the Lord has gone out against me!"*

What started with Adam and Eve ("It's the woman you gave me, God.") is working on Naomi. But, Naomi is a little different—she blames God for her losses! In her mind, obviously, God was punishing her for making wrong choices. The truth is, God never wanted to see them leave in the first place. Just as the Children of Israel experienced famine due to their disobedience, Naomi's losses were the consequences of *her own,* inconsistent decision.

Again, this same pattern of thinking runs rampant in the Church today. By nature, people have a difficult time accepting responsibility for their own actions or decisions. It is too easy to blame God, their church, their family, their boss, or the government while never taking the time to look into the mirror!

Take the workplace, as an example. Too many people, even though they have an undying love for God, have trouble displaying a consistent work ethic. They show up late, underachieve in their performance, have a rotten attitude, and do not receive promotions and raises. While others are being blessed, they are in a famine. All of the sudden they say, *"God is moving me on to a better job where I am respected and paid for my efforts."* But guess what? Without a change of heart and a better work ethic, things will be the same. Maybe even worse!

There is an old adage that says: *"Every time you move, you take the mirror with you!"*

Oh, how true that is! The mirror goes with us every time. And until the person in that mirror changes, the results will be the same. Another hard question to ask yourself is, *"Is this me? Do I blame-shift instead of accepting responsibility for my actions? Am I a victim of my own inconsistency?"*

Maybe you are a victim of your own decision, or you were dealt a bad hand like Naomi's children. Mahlon and Chilion were casualties of bad decisions made generations before them. But, here is the good news: you don't have to die—spiritually or emotionally—because of someone else's inconsistent actions! God in His covenant faithfulness wants to restore your life! What is the path of that restoration?

The power of consistency!

Chapter 4

THE TALE OF TWO LADIES

Consistency Brings Relationships

"And Naomi said to her two daughters-in-law, 'Go, return each to her mother's house. The Lord deal kindly with you, as you have dealt with the dead and with me. The Lord grant that you may find rest, each in the house of her husband.' Then she kissed them, and they lifted up their voices and wept.

Ruth 1:8-9

Naomi has found herself in a very difficult position. Alone, widowed, without her sons, and with two daughter-in-laws trying to return to the place she should have never left. She obviously knew the chances of her re-marrying, becoming pregnant with two more sons; and her daughter-in-laws staying single until those two sons reached the age of marriage, was not a possibility. Hopelessly, Naomi tells her two daughters-in-law to move on with their lives, not to worry about her, and to return to their respective lands and homes. Naomi blessed them, kissed them, and sent them on their way. Orpah took her offer and left. But, Ruth was about to change Naomi's life forever!

> *"Then they lifted up their voices and wept again; and Orpah kissed her mother-in-law, but Ruth clung to her."*
>
> **Ruth 1:14**

The name "Ruth" means *"friend,"* but in a much deeper connotation than we would think. In today's world, a "friend" might be a golfing or fishing buddy, someone to talk to on the phone a few times a week, or maybe a shopping partner. Actually, these types of relationships are more acquaintances. But, Ruth was much deeper than a casual acquaintance; she was in relationship with Naomi. Her name has the concept of *"one who is in covenant relationship with another,"* and a covenant with Naomi is exactly what she committed to.

KISSER OR CLEAVER

There really could not have been two women who were more opposite than Ruth and her mother-in-law. Yet, God chose this relationship to eventually bring restoration to an entire nation.

Naomi had lived in "a place of the 'Word' (Bethlehem)" and experienced a covenant relationship with the Lord God Almighty. Still, throughout her relationship with God, she was plagued with an inconsistent lifestyle. Ruth, on the other hand, was a Moabite. Remember the Moabites? They were a people who were full of seduction and knew nothing about a relationship with God. She probably never went to VBS or summer youth camp, yet she did possess an outstanding characteristic: consistency. This was the vehicle that would become the foundation of her life, bring great recognition, and launch her into her preordained destiny.

Naomi tries once again to convince Ruth that her best life would be to follow in the footsteps of her sister-in-law, Orpah; return back to her country, start all over, and get a new life. Even though this was a viable option, the consistent life and Ruth's covenant heart produced another answer:

> *"But Ruth said: 'Entreat me not to leave you, Or to turn back from following after you; For wherever you go, I will go; And wherever you lodge, I will lodge; Your people shall be my people, And your God, my God. Where you die, I will die, And there will I be buried. The Lord do so to me, and more also, If anything but death parts you and me.'"*
>
> Ruth 1:16-17

Talk about restoration! In today's vernacular, Ruth's answer would have sounded like this:

> *"Naomi, I know you have lived a life of bad decisions, but let me demonstrate to you what restoration looks like! I know you feel like a victim and think God has put this all on*

you, but God brought me to you and I'm staying with you all the way through to death. We are going to break this cycle and watch God do something miraculous in our lives, together!"

Ruth was a "cleaver," committing herself to die with Naomi. It made no difference to her how they were put together, Ruth was not leaving! Orpah, on the other hand, was a "kisser." Not only did she kiss her mother-in-law goodbye, she also kissed away her relationship. "Cleavers" understand longevity and covenant; "kissers" only see what is in their best interest.

There is a major difference between the two!

Covenant relationships—REAL covenant relationships—are very difficult to find and even harder to maintain. Our society has taken, *"I will be with you through thick and thin,"* and dumbed it down to: *"As long as it does not cost me time, money, or reputation...then we can be in relationship."* Did you ever think you would see the day where Internet divorces were cheaper than a pair of shoes? Now, for a mere $79.95, you can legally walk out of your marriage covenant and be free as a bird. As crazy as it sounds, it is the world we live in.

A few years ago, a very famous college football coach moved to become the head coach of a predominant NFL team. After receiving his contract and bonus, one of his first orders of business was to divorce his wife! His reason? In the college world, with boosters, supporters, and the pressure of recruiting, a wife was a social asset that made him and the program "look good." But, now she wasn't necessary! What? Wasn't necessary? This is the equivalent of, "*Well, I had to wear a tie at my other position to make a good impression, but now I'm promoted; and the tie is not necessary!*"

This is the mentality of a "kisser": "*just help me get to where I need to be, and then I'll kiss you goodbye!*"

You can always find "kissers" especially if there is something in it for them! They are the ones who will always "kiss up" to you; but when things go a little awry, they will "kiss off" as quickly as they "kissed up." "Cleavers" are vastly different and few and far between. They are consistent and not wavered by difficult times. "Cleavers" are committed, no matter what the situation, and are very often the catalysts of hope that can help transform a life through a devastating circumstance.

A GREAT WORD SPOKEN IN SEASON

Our very first weekend in Macon was extra special. Some very important people in our lives were in town for a special event, and we had the privilege of spending some time with them. During our time together, they gave us a piece of advice which helped us tremendously. They said, "*Release ministry generously, but release authority slowly.*" I cannot tell you how many times we have reverted back to their counsel, especially when faced with a 'kisser!"

One gentleman, in particular, comes to mind.

This young man had served in some significant leadership roles with other churches, but was intrigued with being a part of helping establish a new church. At first, I thought, "*This is great! God has sent us a qualified person to help!"...that was, until our first phone conversation. Before I could even finish the first "hello," he was off-to-the-races, telling me his church resume and all the good things he could bring to our new work. It was nothing more than a kiss up! All the red flags began to quickly wave, and the advice from our trusted friends came screaming back to me. Politely, yet firmly, I let him know that even though he had been used by God somewhere else, we did not have any positions available at that particular time.

And, he was not the only one! Over the years, we have seen several "kissers" come and go—some with great potential and great gifting. If they did stay, it usually was not for any length of time. At the first sign of conflict or a self-benefiting opportunity, they moved on to greener pastures. This opened our eyes to another very important lesson: relationships that are tested and grow must go through challenges and disagreements. How someone handles conflicts, unmet expectations, and correction will reveal if they are a "kisser" or a "cleaver."

TIME TO GO HOME!

Naomi, with Ruth attached to her side, returned back to her original place—the place of the Word and praise. But, Naomi was not the same person as when she left. There was a noticeable difference. The wrong decision to step out into a foreign land not only affected her family and closest relationships, but it also totally warped her self-worth and self-evaluation. Verse 19 describes her like this:

The Tale of Two Ladies

> *"...when they had come to Bethlehem, that all the city was excited because of them; and the women said, 'Is the Naomi?' But she said to them, 'Do not call me Naomi; call me Mara, for the Almighty has dealt very bitterly with me.'"*
>
> **Ruth 1:19-20**

Can you hear the excitement of the women as they are thrilled to see Naomi?

"Hey, girlfriend, where you been? That little vacation sure turned into a long trip. What happened? Did you get a flat tire? Lose your passport? Ten years is a long, long time. Whatever the case, we are so happy to see you back home."

But Naomi could not share in their excitement. Instead, she quickly instructed the welcoming women to not call her Naomi—which means *"pleasant"*—but to call her "Mara" instead—meaning *"bitter."*

This is still too common with people who leave their God-place! When they return—if they return at all—they are usually very bitter, angry, and calloused. Many unbelievably gifted people have come

> Hurting people need time to heal and need others to be patient with them through the process.

Consistency Brings Relationship | 73

STAY PUT

> ...consistency isn't a spiritual issue as much as it is a character issue!

through our church and when asked to pray about becoming involved in a ministry, they responded, "*Pastor Trey, we would like to, but we got really hurt at our last church, and now we just want to be regular members.*" These people once enjoyed the fruit of service. Unfortunately, their joy has been replaced with resentment and bitterness. Instead of using the gifts God has given them to make an impact on others, they find themselves shrinking back from life and ministry opportunities. In essence, they are a "Naomi"—once pleasant, but now bitter.

The bottom line is, these people are hurting! Hurting people need time to heal and need others to be patient with them through the process. Truthfully, we all need people to be patient with us. Churches are filled with wounded, yet good-hearted, talented, and gifted people who are sitting on the sidelines and are not utilizing their abilities for the Kingdom of God. Even though it is a common scenario, it is also sad and grievous.

DON'T JUMP SHIP

Remember, Naomi's troubles began as just a quick break, a short vacation. It is the same with Christians serving in the Kingdom. Even in the midst of a powerful atmosphere, fatigue can take its toll and result in the decision to pull away for a little space.

Spiritual dryness now gives way to spiritual death. Not just for you, but for the people who are closest to you, as well.

When God has placed you in a particular place with a specific responsibility, stay faithful and consistent. Will there be difficult times? Absolutely. Will everything always be perfect? Probably not. But these challenging times are the opportunities for you to stay steady, firm, and grow. Before you cop an attitude and do something that could be detrimental to your whole family, ask yourself:

"Has God blessed me and my house while serving in this position?"

"Is the revelation of His Word bringing forth fruit?"

"Is God really directing me to leave, or is it just my frustration taking over?"

Again, hard questions—but the truth can help pinpoint your spiritual condition and save you a lot of heartache down the road.

One of the best Old Testament pictures for the New Testament Church is Noah's Ark. Think about it. Here you have a floating building, full of diversity, which God used as an instrument of salvation. It sounds just like the Church today! Although we glamorize the Ark with creative artwork, jewelry, and paintings; there was actually nothing glamorous about it whatsoever. Not one of those animals was supernaturally constipated...for 40 days! (Obviously, this is not a Bible story for the dinner table!) Needless to say, the Ark was, at times, full of mess—just like some churches today.

The animals, however, were a bit different than some church people.

For 40 days, not one of those animals jumped ship! They didn't even ask to be let off at the next port of call! They stuck it out. Mess and all! Why? Because even though it wasn't the perfect surroundings, it was God's perfect place for them.

The Bible describes the Church like this:

> *"But now God has set the members, each one of them, in the body just as He pleased."*
>
> 1 Corinthians 12:18 (NKJV)

Just like the Ark, our perfect place is never going to be perfect. There is no perfect church. No perfect pastor. No perfect worship service. The reason? Because churches are comprised of imperfect people—just like you and me! One of the keys to consistent, covenant life is staying put where God has placed you. Even when it stinks and is messy, do as the animals did—don't jump ship!

Stay pleasant and not bitter.

CONVENIENCE, COVENANT, AND CHARACTER

Have you ever met someone who was solid and reliable, but had very little or no relationship with God? Sure you have. We all have. Then we start to ask, *"How can someone be so consistent, yet not be a very spiritual person?"* And here is the truth: consistency isn't a spiritual issue as much as it is a character issue! Being a Christian is not required for someone to pay their bills on time, have a great work ethic, and stay faithful in their relationships. Now, in no way am I insinuating that all Christians are slackers! This would be preposterous. However, if we take a realistic look, the un-churched—the Moabites—have reaped the benefits of a consistent life sometimes more than the covenant people of God.

What we have come to realize over the years is that real relationships aren't always convenient.

IT ALL WORKS TOGETHER

As for Naomi and Ruth, the foundation of their lives has been laid. Wrong decisions have been made. Tragedy has struck. Self-confidence has been lost. But, through it all, a covenant relationship has been established—one which would last forever, change a nation, and provide incredible benefits to the two ladies who were now committed to each other.

What started as a loss is now about to all change...thanks to the power of consistency!

Chapter 5

WORDS NOT REQUIRED

Consistency Speaks

Whether you believe it or not, our lives are constantly speaking; and our moving lips are not necessarily a pre-requisite! Even when our voices are silent and our lips are still, *our lives speak.* The Bible says there are many voices in the world, and none without significance (1 Corinthians 14:10); but those voices are not always verbal. Actually, many times, things are communicated without one word ever being breathed. Some researchers report that over 75% of all communication is now non-verbal.[1] Attitudes speak. Facial expressions speak. Our commitment—or lack thereof—has a voice. The way we serve and treat our spouses says much about our lives,...and so on.

Over the years, I have had the opportunity to be in several different local church settings. In all of my visits, one thing always stood out: how the church body speaks before the senior pastor ever says one word! The facilities speak. The parking attendants have a voice. Greeters at the door do more than just say,

"Welcome." They set the tone of the entire church body. Cleanliness and excellence always present an attitude about the church. Ushers, children's workers, nursery workers, and the worship team—they ALL speak of the overall function, focus, and general position of the church.

Corporate America has a multitude of voices as well. Have you ever called a business, and the person answering the phone sounded like they hated their job? What response did it generate from you? Probably the same as it does me, *"Why am I going to spend my money with these people?"* Even if their product is the best on the market, if the process to buy it is filled with angry, rude people, you're probably going to find it somewhere else. If you're a business owner or aspire to own a business one day, never lose this concept: your employees speak for you!

And your business has competitors!

Mark Cuban, media mogul, billionaire, and the owner of the Dallas Mavericks basketball team, once posted a blog to reiterate this point. Actually, he conveyed the story of mega-search engine computer giant, Yahoo®. They realize there are other e-mail services vying for their customers, so they make sure their employees understand what every letter in their name means: *You* *A*lways *H*ave *O*ther *O*ptions.[2]

I think it would be well-served if every business, organization, and church were to be reminded of this fact. Without saying a word, we are all communicating. One the loudest voices to be "heard" is:

Consistency!

It was about to speak for Ruth and change her life, forever!

A DIVINE SET-UP

Naomi and Ruth are back in their place—the place of the Word and praise. This time, it was different. God had restored the region and turned their desolation into harvest! The dry season was over, and once again their crops were producing. Even though she was stricken with a generational curse of incest and carried all kinds of emotional baggage, Ruth sees beyond her past and valiantly pursues a God opportunity.

She tells her mother-in-law, *"With all that we've been through together, we surely did not come back to this place to starve to death. Let me go out and do some work. I know I can start in the fields, gleaning after the reapers."* So, Ruth's journey begins, but she had no idea just how God was orchestrating her steps!

> **"There was a relative of Naomi's husband, a man of great wealth, of the family of Elimelech. His name was Boaz.**
>
> **Ruth 2:1**

Enters the scene: Boaz, a relative of Naomi's late husband. Boaz, which means *"swiftness,"* was not just an ordinary, long-lost relative. Instead, he was a man of great wealth and powerful social influence. He was of a very high stature, much like a warrior hero, and was very well known and respected within the community. When Boaz would visit a social event, it wasn't necessary for him take a Sharpie® and write, "Boaz" on a name tag. He was immediately recognized. More importantly, he was part of a divine set-up.

Boaz, like many high-impact people, is surrounded by "kissers." No wonder Ruth immediately grabbed his attention! She was something he was not used to. Ruth was different. Something on the *inside* of her was more powerful than her *outward* natural ability. Eventually, it would be the thing that brought Boaz's blessing and her promotion.

LET'S GET TO WORK

> *"So Ruth the Moabitess said to Naomi, 'Please let me go to the field, and glean heads of grain after him in whose sight I may find favor.' And she said to her, 'Go, my daughter.'"*
>
> Ruth 2:2 (NKJV)

Armed with an unchangeable quest for a better life, Ruth begins her journey to the fields where God was providing a harvest. It was a rebuilding process. Rebuilding is never easy, as it challenges anyone to the core of their beliefs and commitment. One reason rebuilding is such a struggle is because no one starts back at the top—*you start any place you can!*

During this particular time in history, farmers would leave a rationing of wheat and grain at the corners of the harvest field and all along its edges. It was a way to provide for those in need or strangers who might be traveling through the region without any food. Even though this practice does not exist any longer, one thing is same today as then: egos! No one likes to beg for food.

Picking up the left-overs—or gleaning—is not the social status anyone desires. But, when you are starting over and have the need for basic survival, a personal ego becomes secondary.

Ruth was in this very position. Willing to put herself in a position of being destitute, she was thankful to take what was left behind. And, she did it faithfully, consistently, and with undying dedication. What if Ruth would have taken the, *"Wait a minute, I can't do this. It is way beneath me!"* attitude? Better yet, how many times have *we* had that same attitude?

You know the story: God is trying to break us out into a new dimension and the first thing required of us is what we deem "beneath us." In words, actions, or both, we respond, *"Oh, no way, God! That's way too small for me. I wouldn't be using my full talents or capacity."* Or the infamous, *"Get someone who is just starting out to do this. I have way too much expertise and experience!"* Or my personal favorite, *"That's just not my calling!"* I think we need to be reminded of the words of Jesus when He said, "If you are going to be trusted with much, you must first be faithful in the small things" (Matthew 25:23).

Of course, there is someone who is more dangerous than the one who does not participate in the things that are "beneath them." It is the ones who actually *do* accept the assignment, but carry an infectious, horrible attitude! They gripe and complain from the first moment they start. You can be assured that an inconsistent performance is inevitable. Not only does their attitude and words affect them, it also carries over to those surrounded by their misery. Then, they wonder why they find themselves so frustrated and anxious. It is painfully obvious to those looking from the outside, in.

STAY PUT

While other people are receiving raises, promotions, and bonuses, those who have chosen to be ruled by their egos are passed by. Remember, our lives and actions are always speaking; and those of influence are listening. When starting over, the best path to take is the same one Ruth did: *"Lord, nothing is too small for me."*

FROM THE BOTTOM UP

I have a friend who enjoyed many years of fruitful ministry. After leaving his last church staff position, he and his wife unfortunately went through a divorce. Suddenly, he was faced with no position, no ministry, no family, and very little support. Seeing that the ministry was their only source of employment over the last 20 years, it was overwhelming to fathom working a job not ministry-related. But life rolled on, and bills needed to get paid.

> God is setting us up for a divine appointment—one that will launch us into our destiny.

During the ensuing Christmas season, he was offered a job at a department store during the holiday rush. He took the job as a clothing sales associate and performed well—actually, very well. The salary was low, the hours were long, and the emotional drain of coming from an executive ministry position to folding clothes was, at times, almost too much to bear. But, he stuck it out and performed with excellence. In just a few months, he was one of the top producers of the entire store, even though no one ever knew the emotional beating he faced every day.

This particular store drew several upper-end executives and corporate head-hunters. In nine month's time, his excellence and attitude caught their attention! My friend received numerous job offers, one of which he finally accepted. His new boss said, *"If you serve our customers as well as you have served me and my family here at the department store, you will be in good financial shape!"* He wasn't lying! After starting with the new company, he was promoted to a sales position faster than anyone else in the company's 26-year history. And within six months, he began to make *monthly* what he use to make *yearly!*

What would have happened if he would have thought that folding clothes was "beneath his ability"? He would have never been in the position God was designing for him all along.

Consistency speaks! People notice! Influential people are always in search of someone who is committed, reliable, steadfast, and unswerving...even in seemingly menial tasks. And, sometimes, God is setting us up for a divine appointment—one that will launch us into our destiny.

Boaz was just that person for Ruth!

"Then she left, and went and gleaned in the field after the reapers. And she happened to come to the part of the field belonging to Boaz, who was of the family of Elimelech."

Ruth 2:3 (NKJV)

NO MORE LONE RANGER!

There are many, many power aspects to the story of Ruth, one being this very scripture. The Bible says that Ruth "happened" to fall in Boaz's field. Actually, it wasn't happenstance or circumstance at all! It was a divine appointment. Later, we will see all the implications of this one, powerful encounter.

Ruth is not the only person with a predestined place and calling. We all have one! Our particular assignment is designed by God Himself. However, for many years, too many of us have been deceived by the "Lone Ranger" scenario. We have thought, *"If God has ordained a place for me, then He can get me there by myself."* That is true in the sense that God is omnipotent and can make anything happen at anytime. But, there are also laws which govern certain activity. Just look at gravity and inertia. They are laws set into motion by God. There is also a pattern which God set in motion for anyone to reach their ordained destiny in life. It is this: You can only obtain your place in life through relationships and connections!

> You can only obtain your place in life through relationships and connections.

In other words, everyone has to have a Boaz in their life—someone established, reputable, sincere, and influential who can come along and expedite your journey into your destiny! It is a divine set-up and has been the pattern of success for centuries.

There are several, natural keys that expedite these relationships to birth and develop. One is this: high impact people will not gravitate toward inconsistent people. It just does not happen. Why? Because they already know the discipline, character, and fortitude it takes to accomplish success. Eagles do not fly with buzzards, nor do highly trained thoroughbreds run with mules. People who are looking for someone to mentor and train will take consistency and a hard work ethic over talent, *any day!*

This shift is very evident in corporate America. Business leaders are now placing more emphasis on people with *character*, and those who can have good chemistry with others, over *competency*. (Remember, consistency is a result of character, not talent.) They believe it is easier to teach someone to do a job rather than to teach people to have character. People who lie, never show up on time, gossip about their co-workers, and place themselves above the team are finding out the hard way: character beats competency!

BUILDING BLOCKS

How many times have we come to a place in life where we think we just need more stuff? *"My business would take off if I could just get that contract." "My church would grow if I could get that building." "My life would be better if I had more money."* Although contracts, buildings, and money are all important, they are not the building blocks God uses to build a life. What God does use are high impact people who can speak wisdom into our lives. One divine connection from God can bring more contracts, and subsequently more money, than ten marketing campaigns, combined!

These relationships elevate us into our God-ordained destiny.

I can honestly say, Hope and I would not be where we are today if it were not for the relationships God has orchestrated. We have never looked at divine relationships as God punching our ticket to success. They have much deeper meaning and significance. These voices build character and wisdom into our lives and prepare us to not squander future opportunities. The first step is being consistent over a period of time with the relationships God ordains.

One thing I have learned is that I need more wisdom than stuff. Can God use a divine connection to open doors of opportunity? Absolutely. But, that is not their primary function. The number one reason God places significant people in our lives is to shape our character. In the right time, doors will open.

ACTIONS DO THE SELLING

Ruth was in the right place serving the right person. A God-connection. As well, her life was already speaking to Boaz, and he was taking notice!

> *"Then Boaz said to his servant who was in charge of the reapers, 'Whose young woman is this?' So the servant who was in charge of the reapers answered and said, 'It is the young Moabite woman who came back with Naomi from the country of Moab. And she said, "Please let me glean and gather after the reapers among the sheaves."*

So she came and has continued from morning until now, though she rested a little in the house.'"

Ruth 2:5-7

Up until this moment, Ruth has never uttered one word to Boaz. Not one conversation, coffee meeting, e-mail, or luncheon. Not a word. But, something else was speaking for her—her consistent work ethic! This is the message it declared:

"That's Ruth, the Moabite girl who came back with Naomi. She arrives early in the morning, works hard all day, and never complains. She took a little rest but came right back to work with the same great attitude and results!"

Now, I don't know about you, but if I'm in Boaz's position, that would be the *exact* type of person I would notice and promote! Someone who works hard with no recognition. Someone who is not selling themselves with their mouths, but is letting their actions and results do the talking! Someone who is asking, *"Where can I help? What can I do?"* instead of always insisting, *"Your company would be so fortunate to have me!"* Words fade quickly, while actions speak volumes!

OPPORTUNITIES, NOT MIRACLES

As a senior pastor, I often counsel people who are changing careers, have been recently laid off due to down-sizing, or are re-entering the workforce. I always ask them these questions: *"How many resumes* have you sent out?" "How many phone calls or visits to prospective employers?" "Have you searched the Internet, hired a head-hunter, or made yourself available through each and every medium possible?" Their answers usually locate their level of commitment.

It never ceases to amaze me how many times I hear, "*Well, I am praying and believing God for a miracle. If God fed the children of Israel, then He will bring manna to my door.*" Undoubtedly, God does get involved in these situations, but it is usually AFTER the process has begun. At the risk of being offensive, I tell them, "Most people need to stop asking for miracles and start looking for opportunities!"

About that time, our counseling session is usually finished!

> **Most people need to stop asking for miracles and start looking for opportunities!**

There is a gentleman in our church who lost his job because of corporate down-sizing. Immediately, he began sending out numerous resumes and worked hard to find new employment. One day, he heard the Lord tell him to go to the Department of Labor and tell them that he was tired of getting paid unemployment for doing nothing. Now that takes faith! He then volunteered his time every week to teach many of the young men who were enrolled in basic life-skill classes. He wasn't looking for a miracle; he found an opportunity. The results? This man did find a great new job where he is prospering and developing.

When we begin to walk in the God-given opportunities—no matter how insignificant they may seem—God will release favor into our lives to bring increase, blessing, and promotion!

NOW, THE REAL TESTS!

What could be better for Ruth? Her diligence has gained her an invitation from one of the most predominate men in the region. Of course, if she was like most of us, she probably would be thinking, *"Hey, maybe Boaz is going to offer me a position of notoriety. Maybe all my hard work is about to pay off. This is my day, my moment!"* But again, Ruth is not like most of us!

> *"Then Boaz said to Ruth, 'You will listen, my daughter, will you not? Do not go to glean in another field, nor go from here, but stay close by my young women. Let your eyes be on the field which they reap, and go after them. Have I not commanded the young men not to touch you? And when you are thirsty, go to the vessels and drink from what the young men have drawn.'"*
>
> **Ruth 2:8-9**

Access had been granted. Now, the real tests begin! Even if it was not what Ruth was *expecting*, it was exactly what she *needed*.

Why the tests? What exactly was Boaz looking to find? Was he looking to expose any negative reactions? No, quite the opposite. He was giving opportunity for Ruth's positive characteristics to surface. Knowing that she was destined for much more than just gleaning the fields, he needed to know particular things like:

Can she follow instructions?

Can she be consistent in submitting?

Was her character full of integrity?

Can she be trusted with larger tasks and responsibilities?

Will she run from difficulties?

The process was not complicated. It simply consisted of back-breaking work—gathering, carrying, and harvesting sheaves of wheat and bags of seed. Definitely not the most prestigious job in the city. The work was laborious. Night after night, Ruth went home, exhausted. Monotony and boredom had surely set in. The process was in full gear, but there was more happening than what met the eye. Boaz was not attempting just to get work *out of her*; more importantly, he was also imparting things *into her*.

Ruth was now learning to value what Boaz valued. She was becoming accustomed to the culture of his household. In the bigger picture, these tests were allowing Ruth to find out more about *herself!* The field of testing will always teach us more about ourselves. Tests can show how we are stronger, tougher, and more courageous than we ever imagined. The process is painful, but the results can be life-changing.

According to the Bible, Boaz had two main areas of concern which Ruth needed to display the right answers and attitude. Amazingly, these same two characteristics are sought after by today's CEOs and business executives.

TEST #1
Can You Listen and Follow Instructions?

"Then Boaz said to Ruth, 'You will listen, my daughter, will you not?'"

Ruth 2:8a

Successful people have many things in common. Two of them are: (1.) they listen, and (2.) they remain teachable. Boaz knows how important these two qualities are, so he wastes no time in getting to the foundation of Ruth's character. He needed to know how she responds to authority. Will she listen and follow instructions or rebel with insubordination?

Have you ever known someone who gives mental ascent to every instruction they are told, but rarely follows through? Following instructions is elementary; but for some, it is a constant struggle. Being teachable is much more than just hearing information and nodding in agreement; it is proven through corresponding actions. First, we have to listen. Listening is hearing for understanding. Once understanding is achieved, then we must act on what we have heard. Those who remain teachable will be consistent learners, and those who follow instructions will always position themselves for promotion.

> **TEST # 2**
>
> Can You Function Within Boundaries?

"Do not go to glean in another field, nor go from here, but stay close by my young women."

Ruth 2:8b

Right after "listening" comes limitations. Boundaries. Borders. The kind of stuff that drives you crazy, but all are a major tests of character. Of course, some people would say, *"How dare Boaz put restrictions on that hard-working Ruth! Who is he to tell her which field she can work in? He's just trying to box her in and keep her down!"* Can't you just see the Bethlehem-Judah Employment Commission starting to file their formal complaint? But this was far more than just a requirement; it was a test of self-will.

The reason this was such an important issue to Boaz was due to Ruth's background. Remember, she was a foreigner from Moab with a dysfunctional family history. Many counselors agree that dysfunctional people do not properly understand boundaries or respect the personal space of others. They have a tendency to intrude and constantly move from one place to another with very little commitment. Knowing her Moabite lineage, Boaz's concern was clear: can Ruth be committed to *his field* on *his terms*? Can she be committed? Will she be consistent when the new wears off?

Little did Ruth know that her ability to follow instructions and work within the framework given to her was laying the groundwork to take her life into a whole different dimension.

A life she had never dreamed of!

THE WAY TO PROMOTION

One of the greatest joys of being a leader is watching people follow instructions and do what they say they will do! It sounds simple, doesn't it? But, it is not as easy as it sounds. Those who do not follow instructions are inconsistent and overstep boundaries; they are under-committed and are not candidates for promotion. Jesus had to deal with these same issues even with those closest to Him.

In the New Testament, Jesus asked His disciples many times, *"Why can't you guys get it?"* In John Chapter 14, He made it plain: the proof of their love for Him was how they obeyed—*both hearing and doing*—what He had taught. Was Jesus being too harsh and unfair to His followers? No. In actuality, He was paving the way to completely turn His entire ministry over to His disciples. They needed to be ready for such a responsibility.

> We all need to learn to be consistent listeners, people who follow instructions, and are submitted to God's authority.

In the same way, Boaz was preparing Ruth for the future. The tests in the field were just part of the preparation process. The same is true in our lives. We all need to learn to be consistent listeners, people who follow instructions, and are submitted to God's authority. Boundaries are not set in place to limit our effectiveness and rain on our parade. They are there to test our commitment and break our self-will. They also define a realm of opportunity. It is all part of the process which draws us closer to Him and prepares us for what lies ahead.

Whether you have been in this field of testing many times or for the first time, choose to follow the path of consistency. Stay faithful in the testing. Look at the bigger picture of what you are learning about *yourself*. The field may be painful, but the results can be supernatural!

Just like Ruth is about to experience!

"The way to gain a good reputation is to endeavor to be what you desire to appear."

— Socrates

Chapter 6

A GOOD NAME AND SO MUCH MORE

Consistency Brings Reputation and Favor

We have all heard the expression, *"Your reputation has preceded you."* As cliché as it might sound, it is still very much a fact. For some, it is a great precursor and introduction; for others, it is a blinking red light which says, *"Stay away. Beware!"*

Here's the good news: according to the Bible, when you establish a good name—a good reputation—riches, relationships, and opportunities seem to follow!

"A good name is to be chosen rather than great riches, loving favor rather than silver and gold."

Proverbs 22:1

Reputations—both good and bad—speak. Restaurant owners now believe the customers who had a bad experience will tell 10 people, while a good meal and good service might only be conveyed to two or three. This is why they spend countless hours and

STAY PUT

> ...favor is the key ingredient for sustained increase and blessing.

thousands of dollars each year training their staff. No longer is just serving good food sufficient. Now, employees must know how to properly greet and serve guests, anticipate the needs of their patrons, and know how to handle conflict in a way that will honor the customer and earn their favor. In short, a good restaurant "experience" is now the goal.

The same is true for our lives. Every day, we are a walking, living "experience," and someone around us is examining our life. So, we should consistently be asking ourselves:

"Is my 'experience' a good one? Am I positive and making a good, lasting impression on those around me? Is my reputation such that people want to risk their time, money, and opportunities with me?"

These might be hard questions, but the honest answers are very revealing.

THE ULTIMATE REWARD

Of course, Ruth's "life experience" was speaking...and speaking loud! Her reputation had indeed preceded her, and her life of consistency was passing the tests set before her. Now, it was time to reap some benefits; one in particular—favor.

> *"So she fell on her face, bowed down to the ground, and said to him, 'Why have I found favor in your eyes, that you should take notice of me, since I am a foreigner?'"*
>
> **Ruth 2:10-13**

Here is another very interesting detail in Ruth's journey. When she was preparing to leave Naomi and work in fields, she said these words:

> *"...Please let me go to the field... in whose sight I may find favor..."*
>
> **Ruth 2:2 (NKJV)**

Notice, her ultimate goal was not to find *food*, but *favor*! Why favor? Because food is only a means of survival; but favor is the key ingredient for sustained increase and blessing. It is like the old saying which says, *"Give a man a fish, and he will eat. Teach him how to fish, and he will never go hungry again."* All of her hard work, all of the testing, and all of the humiliation mixed with Ruth's consistent lifestyle was now bringing her desired goal:

FAVOR!

And what was Boaz's response? Just what she was waiting to hear!

> *"And Boaz answered and said to her, 'It has been fully*

> *reported to me, all that you have done for your mother-in-law since the death of your husband, and how you have left your father and your mother and the land of your birth, and have come to a people whom you did not know before. The Lord repay your work, and a full reward be given you by the Lord God of Israel, under whose wings you have come for refuge.'"*
>
> Ruth 2:11-12 (NKJV)

Ruth's outstanding reputation was as follows: she was a person who could be trusted, a person of character and virtue, and someone who gave generously to others and was not selfish. What if she was someone who was always trying to push her way in the door? Or bossy? Or lazy? Believe me, those characteristics would have grabbed Boaz's attention, as well, and produced less than desirable results.

The world is full of people who act one way to get noticed and promoted; but as soon as they get their "break," the real person comes out! They become eaten up with pride and carry an attitude of entitlement. Their heart to serve changes to, *"I'm all that...and then some!"* Sadly, when they become unthankful for their opportunities, the blessing of favor is usually short-lived. The best way to respond when your reputation allows God to open a door of opportunity is in humility. Just like Ruth.

> *"Then she said, 'Let me find favor in your sight, my lord; for you have comforted me, and have spoken kindly to your*

maidservant, though I am not like one of your maidservants.'"

Ruth 2:13

Humility and thankfulness will keep the door of favor and blessing open.

JUST BECAUSE GOD LIKES US

Even though we hear a lot about the term "favor," we sometimes do not understand its full meaning and capacity. Actually, we use the concept quite often in everyday life. Think about how many times you have asked someone, *"Hey, can you do me a favor?"* It happens all the time. What we are really asking is for that person—usually one we have a relationship with—to do something for us as an act of goodwill or kindness. Most of the time, "favors" are not remunerated and come with no-strings-attached. It is out of the goodness of their heart.

It is the same way with the favor of God!

Now, I'm going to say something here that could potentially upset the applecart of your theology, so hang on! In the Scriptures, it is very evident that God loves *every person on this planet*. John 3:16 says, *"For God so loved the world."* That is an established, non-changing fact. But, there is another trait of God. Even though God *loves* everyone, there are some that He really, really *likes*! This, my friend, is called favor!

You might be saying, *"Wait a minute, that's not fair. Isn't God a fair God?"* Actually, the Bible never says God is fair; but rather, He is just.

> *"For exaltation comes neither from the east, nor from the west, nor from the south. But God is the Judge: He puts down one, and exalts another."*
>
> **Psalm 75:6-8**

Finding favor with God is not a new concept. It happened all throughout the Bible. For example:

- Mary, the teenage virgin, was favored by God and brought forth Jesus into this earth. (Luke 1:46-48)

- God granted the apostles and early disciples favor with man. (Acts 2:46-47)

- King David walked in the favor of God. (1 and 2 Samuel and 1 Chronicles.)

- Even Jesus Himself increased and walked in both the favor of God and men. (Luke 2:52)

The Bible says Jesus increased in favor. It was ever-expanding in His life. This word "increased" is used by metal workers to describe the process of lengthening a piece of metal by pounding it with a hammer. What this means is, as Jesus grew in wisdom and stature, His character was being hammered out as well.

It doesn't matter who you are, working out issues in your life is never easy, but it is a requirement in order to walk in favor with God and with man. It might be tough some days. We may not always get our way. We may have to stand a little pain. But in the end, we are positioned for increase, just like Jesus.

Ruth's tests were not easy, but the outcome was well worth it! In the same way, when we go through some hammering of our character, it gets God's attention and ultimately, his favor!

> ...working out issues in your life is never easy, but it is a requirement in order to walk in favor with God and with man.

> *"The eyes of the Lord run to and fro throughout the whole earth, to show Himself strong on behalf of those whose hearts are loyal to Him."*
>
> 2 Chronicles 16:9

SENIOR GARBAGE DISPOAL TECHNICIAN

Hope and I learned early on in our marriage that when God is smiling your way, you are in pretty good shape! We have experienced this many times during our life. Once was when we were trying to find our way as a newly married couple.

While we attended undergraduate school, both of our parents were very gracious to provide for our education and needs. We were truly blessed. But, in between my first and second semesters of graduate school, we decided to get married. It was a new season. With new responsibilities! Right after we married, God spoke to my heart to enroll in Regent University. What could be better? We were in marital bliss, I had heard and obeyed God's voice, and we were "living on love."

Then, reality raised its ugly head!

My first semester at Regent, I worked some odd jobs, but we needed more money to support the two of us. Hope was also looking for a job since my time was heavily invested in graduate school. We also needed a place to live, so I put in an application for an apartment at the university's student housing complex. The lady who worked there was a fellow student whom I had met at one of my odd jobs during the first semester. She initially told me that there were no vacancies. The very next day, she called and told us an apartment was coming available, *and* we had been bumped up to the front of the waiting list. It was just what we needed.

> ...no one is called to everybody, but everyone is called to somebody.

After we moved in, I went back into the housing office to ask about employment. Much to my surprise, this same lady was no longer just a secretary; she was running the entire complex! She immediately gave me a job for 20 hours a week working as the apartment's maintenance assistant. Basically, I was a glorified toilet plunger, grass cutter, light bulb changer, and garbage disposal technician. In any case, this was a major blessing! Now, I could continue to go to school full-time, work, have a place to live; and Hope had the car to go to work as I used the university's shuttle to class.

We were already learning how good, consistent decisions were opening God's favor on our lives. Hope had landed a job at CBN, I was working hard in school and at work, and we were both consistently involved in a local church. After the first year on my job, I was offered a promotion to maintenance supervisor—which simply meant I was now the *head* toilet plunger, grass cutter, light bulb changer, and senior garbage disposal technician! It also meant more hours and more income, which we were very thankful for. I began to work 40 hours a week; plus, we were provided a three-bedroom apartment, full health coverage, and 75% off my tuition! God was once again shining His face on us.

But, it wasn't the end!

Within the first week on my new job, the University Vice President, who was over student housing, came by to see the changes I had made to my office and shop. He liked it so much that he immediately gave me a $1,000 raise and two new employees to help carry the workload! We were growing in favor with God *and* man. A few years later, I graduated Regent University with honors, had very little school debt, and left with many experiences and lessons learned.

During those first years, things were not always easy and did not always happen the way we planned. Many times, we felt the "hammering out" process was more than we could bear. But, it was all part of the "increasing" process. One of the foundational lessons we learned was the power of consistency. Over and over again, this one element positioned us for God to unexpectedly show up and do something beyond our wildest dreams.

Just because He liked us!

THE LIFE OF FAVOR

When God shines His favor on us, things start to happen! Just look at Ruth. Her reputation not only awarded her favor with God and man, it was about to move her into a totally different dimension of life. Here are five things that favor provided for Ruth and will provide for anyone else who pass the "hammering" tests!

FAVOR OPENS DOORS

"Now Boaz said to her at mealtime, 'Come here, and eat of the bread, and dip your piece of bread in the vinegar.'"

Ruth 2:14a

By now, Boaz is convinced Ruth is "the real deal," even though she is an outsider and does not fit the mold of his maidservants. She had earned his trust; so much so that she was given a place at the table not made available for any other worker.

And, this was not just a regular meal.

When someone would take bread and dip it in the oil, it was a sign of a *covenant meal*. This meant Boaz was now inviting her into a relationship! His perception of her was drastically changing. No longer was she just a gleaner in the field in his eyes, but someone he was willing to invest his life into. His actions broke every barrier and clearly separated Ruth from all the others in the room. Favor was at work!

One of the true signs of a consistent life is how you react once favor opens the door! Sometimes, it is easier to be consistent during a struggle. Then, when the signs of relief appear, it's tempting to just coast and say, *"The hard work has paid off. It's party time!"* This is a sure sign that doors of opportunity will not remain open for long! Ruth's response was just the opposite. There was no way she was going to let inconsistency now take over just as things were getting good! After finishing her covenant meal, this is what she did:

> **"So she sat beside the reapers, and he passed parched grain to her; and she ate and was satisfied, and kept some back."**
>
> **Ruth 2:14b**

She put some of her blessing in reserve and prepared to hit the fields again. Consistency in action. Everything was changing *around her*, but it did not change what was *in her*!

FAVOR BRINGS PROMOTION

"And when she rose up to glean, Boaz commanded his young men, saying, 'Let her glean even among the sheaves, and do not reproach her.'"

Ruth 2:15

Remember the test of boundaries? Ruth passed with flying colors! Not only has her status changed from an outsider to an insider, her boundaries were increasing, as well. No longer would she glean from the scraps on the corner. Now, she had access to the entire field. It is called promotion—or better yet, *increased opportunities*!

Promotion does not come from the north, the south, the east or the west; promotion comes from God. It is the result of a divine pattern which begins with being joined to the right relationships and connections. Understand this truth: no one is called to everybody, but everyone is called to somebody. Favor and promotion follow those who are committed and connected, not jumping from one relationship to another. Today, those people are few and far between.

We live in a *"I'm looking out for number one"* society. Recently, the television show *60 Minutes*, produced a story on the 80 million people born between 1980 and 1995. They are called the Millennials. This group of young adults, by large, were described as being "committed to themselves." Documents proved that their resumes contained four or five jobs per year. Not in their lifespan. Four or five jobs...*every* year. This is a major breakdown of commitment.

And they wonder why they never get promoted!

The Millennials are not unique. Previous generations have had their fair share of inconsistency, as well. Like monkeys swinging from trees, they jumped from place to place, and relationship to relationship. Of course, many are deceived that trading in one relationship for the next is actually promotion! Not so. If anything, it is merely self-promotion and is usually short-lived.

JUST HOLD ME UP!

Every large construction site uses equipment called scaffolding to support the workers while they perform their work above the ground. It is called scaffolding. Although it is an important part of the building process, the scaffolds usually go unnoticed. When the construction crew is finished, they tear them down and move on to the next project. Basically, their only function is to lift someone up and then be moved out when no longer needed.

Sadly, the same is true with relationships!

> One of the true signs of a consistent life is how you react once favor opens the door!

STAY PUT

People seem to concentrate more on the temporary, relationships than those which are substantive and built to last. In short, those "scaffolding" commitments only exist for two reasons: to support their cause and move them up the ladder of "success." And just like the construction workers, when the scaffolding is finished and has completed its job, it is removed and packed away into obscurity. The major difference is that people, unlike scaffolds, are not made of metal! In the end, someone gets hurt and feels used.

You would think these types of relationships just happen in the secular world, right? Wrong. They run rampant in the church world, as well, even with those who are in spiritual authority. Take, for instance, the autocratic pastor who simply views people for his personal gain. The congregation is nothing more than a means to accomplish his "vision," which is usually a combination of his ego covered with the necessary spiritual overtones. These types of leaders are quick to tell everyone else how they should live their lives, but never invite anyone into *their* life for accountability and/or guidance. They are dominated by insecurity, thus the need to control everyone around him; never empowering them to do what they are called, by God, to do. In a nutshell, this is nothing short of spiritual manipulation. It is a spiritual, "scaffolding"

> ...the same consistent life that brought promotion, protection and increase, will also open the door for greater levels of blessing.

relationship, with self-promotion as the end goal. The fruit of this type of relationship has no longevity and usually never lasts more than one generation.

Jesus, on the other hand, was the complete opposite.

He never engaged in fruitless, scaffolding relationships. His vision was not about Himself, but rather the people He served. Jesus chose to be touchable and empowered people to do even *greater things than He did*. In the end, He was promoted. Today, His name holds more authority than any other name that has ever existed. This is real, genuine favor and promotion...*from God*!

THE REAL KEY TO PROMOTION

While favor provides a doorway of promotion, there is a key that unlocks the door. Relationships! It is the way God has designed it to work. Divine relationships help to bring our divine purpose in life to fruition. But, real relationships take work...and a lot of it! The Bible says it like this:

> *"Behold, how good and how pleasant it is for brethren to dwell together in unity... For there the Lord commanded the blessing—life forevermore."*
>
> **Psalm 133:1, 3 (NKJV)**

Notice the words: *"dwell together."* It's not, "*where people tolerate each other,*" or "*where people use each other,*" or "*where relationships are dictated by handbooks, business meetings, or*

Pixie dust only exists in the Magic Kingdom®, not in the Kingdom of God! If we desire change—a real, lasting, noticeable lifestyle change—it will most likely be in the decisions we make to cooperate with God and live a more consistent life of consecration and obedience to Him. Real change is a product of His grace received through trust and intimacy with Him.

WHAT YOU SOW...

The law of sowing and reaping has mainly been related to money. Don't get me wrong, it absolutely works with finances, but it is a law—and laws work in *any* given circumstance.

For example, the law of gravity works, whether you throw a penny in the air or jump out of an airplane. Jesus said if you want to be shown mercy, then you must be merciful towards people. Even the Golden Rule we all learned in grade school is the law of sowing and reaping—do good to others, and someone will do good to you.

Believe me, Ruth has sown...and sown big! Now, the law is working on her behalf. It is time to reap!

> *"Now it is true that I am a close relative; however, there is a relative closer than I. Stay this night, and in the morning it shall be that if he will perform the duty of a close relative for you--good; let him do it. But if he does not want to perform the duty for you, then I will perform the duty for you, as the Lord lives! Lie down until morning."*
>
> **Ruth 3:12-13**

Another mouth-full of promise and blessing from Boaz. But why wait until now to bless her? He knew his kinsman relationship to her the entire time she labored in the fields. Boaz could have used his position of authority to rescue her from long days of toil. But, there was something larger happening in Ruth's life: the development of her character! Sure, a bailout would have relieved some of her pressure, but it would have been short-lived. What she needed was deep-rooted consistency to ensure her success for the overall, bigger picture. She needed to sow character, and she reaped what she sowed.

Character and integrity.

From the person she needed it from the most.

A MAN OF HONOR

How easy would it have been for Boaz to take advantage of this young girl's vulnerability? Instead, his integrity dictates his decisions.

> *"So she lay at his feet until morning, and she arose before one could recognize another. Then he said, 'Don't let it be known that this woman came to the threshing floor.'"*
>
> **Ruth 3:14**

Boaz superseded his own personal needs and lust to make sure Ruth and her mother-in-law were fully restored and exonerated from everything they had lost or had stolen from them. (There is a difference between lost and stolen, and God restores

STAY PUT

votes." No! To *"dwell"* means you remain and stay put! You hammer some things out and dedicate yourself to real, long-term relationships. That is the place where God commands His blessing and favor.

Unlike her sister-in-law, dwelling was the key that launched Ruth into promotion. Her commitment to stay with Naomi—to stick it out through thick and thin—began the process of God's commanded blessing and favor! It was a real, heartfelt commitment.

How ironic is it that we live in a world designed to make relationships easier to attain, yet we grow farther and farther apart? Information can be sent around the world with the push of one "send" button. Global travel is easier now than ever. The issue is while the communication is more readily available, the commitment is sorely lacking.

Now, more than ever, we truly need to ask God for discernment to rightly recognize the divine relationships He has established for our lives. These are the ones that increase in value over time and provide a place of security, rest, and the ability for us to be real and open. This is the place where favor and blessing will find us!

FAVOR PROVIDES PROTECTION

> *"Let her glean even among the sheaves, and do not reproach her."*
>
> **Ruth 2:15**

Here's a newsflash: whenever God's favor is on someone and promotion follows, not everybody will be happy about it! Very few will rejoice with the one who is moving up. In fact, most relationships are severely tested when someone is walking in favor and promotion. Such was the case with Ruth. Obviously, not everyone was happy about this "outsider" catching Boaz's attention and promotion. But, favor also provides divine protection!

By Boaz's command, Ruth was irreproachable. In other words, no one was to rebuke, insult, shame, or humiliate her in any way. She was protected, sheltered, and shielded. The Bible says this is *exactly* what the favor of God does for us. Look at this scripture:

> *"For You, O Lord, will bless the righteous; with favor you will surround him as with a shield."*
>
> **Psalm 5:12**

Favor brings divine protection! We are completely surrounded by the fortress of God! We are covered on all sides. What this means is not only are we shielded from the attacks we can see, but also from the ones we cannot. The "pot shots" people will take—the schemes, lies, and evil plans—from our blind side will not affect us! Consistency brings favor and promotion, and that same favor provides a hand of protection!

FAVOR BRINGS INCREASE

"Also let grain from the bundles fall purposely for her; leave it that she may glean, and do not rebuke her. So she gleaned in the field until evening, and beat out what she had gleaned, and it was about an ephah of barley."

Ruth 2:16-17

With her new position, Ruth is bringing home a full bushel of grain at the end of each day's work. That is definitely more than she would have harvested from just the corners of the field. It is called increase! But, notice *how* this increase was coming about: *people were now working for her!* Now, divine favor was now causing two things to happen to Ruth:

- Her amount of harvest was increasing.

- Her workload was easier than ever!

Favor affects every aspect of our lives. Increase is just one of the ways we can see favor in action. Not that God will rain down $100 bills on our heads—of course, He could if He wanted to!—but He can instruct other people to bless us and make our toil easier. Favor increases us from areas of lack and "just enough" to God's place of abundance and "more than enough."

We love it when God shines His favor and increase on us! It's like walking in a totally different world and environment. But, there is a temptation we must be aware of. It is the danger of pursuing the wrong thing—even for good reasons and motives. If we are not careful, some of these things will get our eyes off of God's provision and cause us to waiver in our consistency towards Him.

There have been times in our ministry where this was the case. In some efforts to raise funds, we did what seemed very normal—sent letters and made videos. Even though these were good communication tools which explained our vision and need, we never saw the return we desired for all of our "hard work." What we failed to realize was that while we were busy putting together all of the fund-raising tools, it caused us to be inconsistent in the things God had called us to do. God had called us into the *people-building* business, not the *fundraising* business! We caught it and made the adjustment—quickly. We began to earnestly seek first the things God had assigned to our lives; and then, it became His job to pay the tab.

And He did!

Touching the heart of God—just as Ruth touched something in Boaz's heart—demonstrates we value what He values, and it releases His favor and increase. Then, the bigger issue arises:

"Can we be consistent in the time of increase?"

When things start to go right, do we have the character to remain consistent in our dedication to what God has called us to?

It is a test of true character. We need to always remember that the same consistent life that brought promotion, protection and increase, will also open the door for greater levels of blessing.

> **FAVOR GIVES YOU A STORY TO TELL**

"Then she took it up and went into the city, and her mother-in-law saw what she had gleaned... And her mother-in-law said to her, 'Where have you gleaned today? And where did you work? Blessed be the one who took notice of you.' So she told her mother-in-law with whom she had worked, and said, 'The man's name with whom I worked today is Boaz.'"

Ruth 2:18,19

Can't you just hear Naomi's words, "*My God, Ruth, where did all of that come from? Who in the world helped you? This is amazing! Tell me all about it!*" Ruth's testimony was more than just of a hard day's work, a sore back, and some blistered hands. Her story was one of hope, opportunities, and future possibilities.

It was the story of divine favor!

TELL YOUR STORY!

One of the most important aspects of experiencing God's favor is telling someone else about it. Our lives should be so full of favor, others stop and ask, *"Hey, what's going on with you?"* At that moment, our lives become an appetizer for those who hunger and thirst for all God has in store for them. And it is not just for those around us; but, more importantly, for those who will follow us! Many times, we fail to see the significance.

We need to ask ourselves, *"How are we supposed to build a legacy of consistency and favor if no one ever hears about it?"* The answer is obvious: we can't! Our future generations need to hear *our* story of open doors, promotion, protection, and increase—not the echoes of someone we knew or heard about. It is all part of establishing a legacy. The Psalmist, David, said it like this:

> *"...that they should make them known to their children...that they may set their hope in God, and not forget the works of God..."*
>
> **Psalms 78:5,7**

Future generations will never know the "works of God" if there are no stories to tell. Think about it. Here we are, thousands of years later, drawing life-lessons from the story of Ruth! It is the power of sharing what God has done; and we must continue to share it. Generations to follow need to hear how consistency can release the favor and blessing of God on their lives, just like it did ours.

THIS ALL STARTED...

...by one, simple request. Ruth asked for favor. Little did she know what was included in the whole package! An open door to a covenant meal. Promotion brought on by a divine relationship. Supernatural protection and increase. Now, she had her own story to tell—the story of God's faithfulness and goodness!

But, back up even further. How did all of this favor and blessing come to her life? The same way it comes to you and me.

From a good reputation.

And a life of consistency.

Chapter 7

DON'T JUST STAND THERE AND STARE

Consistency Makes a Way

The year 2006 was a very pivotal time in our lives. While the church continued meeting in a rented, un-air-conditioned school gymnasium, we desperately needed to find our own building. We felt it was a "do or die" situation, so we began to move forward with architectural drawings for our first building.

The general contractor attended the church, so we were able to get a bid for the total project. Another gentleman in the church, a commercial banker, told me most lending institutions would require our debt-to-income ratio be no more than 40%. At that particular time, we were not close to that target. Our monthly income had to increase for us to qualify for financing, so we started a 12-month campaign. The people were faithful and their giving increased our income to be right at the 40% ratio we needed. We were ready. After reviewing several lending options, we chose the best one and submitted our application.

Dreams and visions of our new building were now racing through my head! The thought of not having to set up and break down every service! Children's facilities! Classrooms! Offices! And, air conditioning to boot! I was shouting, "*Yes, Lord. Bring it on!*"

Then, came the news we were not expecting to hear.

You can only imagine how surprised we were to find out that from the time we had talked to them until now, which had been 12 months, the lending institutions changed their debt-to-income ratio standards! So, instead of 40%, it was now a 30% debt-to-income split! (Of course, this wonderful news came on the day our church loan committee was scheduled to meet.) My stomach was tied into knots. I knew how excited the church was, and I did not think we could handle a disappointment or setback of this magnitude. Two thoughts immediately entered into my mind:

"What will I say to the people who have sacrificially given for us to take this next step?" and, *"If this does not happen, we are sunk!"*

Later the same afternoon, I received a phone call from a gentleman who sat on our lender's loan committee. He began to give me a play-by-play account concerning the status of our application. It seemed that after reviewing our application and church history, all of the loan committee members, including one of the bank's board members, wanted to make the loan work; but our debt-to-income ratio was prohibiting any action.

After a long discussion, this man told me the room fell completely silent.

A few minutes went by, and finally, the board member spoke up and said, *"We all know the three C's in lending—collateral, cash flow and character. This church has the collateral, but not the cash flow. However, I believe the character, faithfulness, and consistency they have demonstrated by not giving up is more important than the cash flow. Let's approve this loan!"* Immediately, the atmosphere went from disappointment to excitement. The man I was speaking with said, *"Trey, it was a miracle!"* The church's character was stronger than our cash flow—or the lack thereof!

God gave us favor! I'm convinced it was not by accident. It was perpetuated by the consistent faithfulness of people who set up chairs, sound systems, swept floors, and cleaned toilets in a hot gym, every week for five years. The lesson learned was this: we did not have to beg or plead; we just had to be consistent.

Faithfulness in hard times had given us a good reputation and eventually brought us favor. Some thought we should just kick back and say, *"Look what the Lord has done!"* Even though we did rejoice for God's favor and faithfulness, we never stopped moving forward. This was not the end of our journey, but merely the entrance. It was the beginning of our destiny, and we knew we just could not stand there and stare! It was time to walk through the door and start affecting other lives that were around us.

How interesting. That's the exact same thing Ruth did!

A COMPLETE 180

Naomi's, Ruth's mother-in-law, has been decimated by disasters. Her entire outlook on life and herself was completely changed.

Even though she was in a legitimate cycle of grief, she has fallen prey to the "victim" mentality. Once a pleasant lady, she has now been overtaken by thoughts like:

> *"I'm hurt. I'm mad. Nothing's working right. God owes me. People have let me down. If you only knew how I've been hurt. If you only knew the challenges and the difficulty I've seen. Nobody understands the pain I'm going through."*

And these thoughts have not changed. Today, they still wage war on those who have found themselves in tough circumstances. But, Naomi had a hope for her sanity and future—her covenant daughter-in-law. Now, Ruth's life of consistency and blessing were going to the next level of influence which, in turn, would pay higher dividends. She was about to reconstruct an entirely new atmosphere for her distraught, beloved mother-in-law.

> **"Then Naomi her mother-in-law said to her, 'My daughter, shall I not seek security for you ..."**

Ruth 3:1

Almost in a blink of any eye, Naomi has changed her focus! *"Poor, little ol' me,"* has changed to *"Let me watch out for your well-being."* What caused this seemingly overnight new outlook on life? As much as we would like to think is was some super-spiritual manifestation, it was not. In fact, it was something very natural. The catalyst for Naomi's change was the consistency of Ruth's life. Not only was she living in the benefits of favor and blessing, now she was also disarming the hopelessness and despondency which had played havoc in mother-in-law's life.

And the proof was evident.

A NEW NAME

It wasn't that long ago that Naomi told Ruth to move to her homeland and begin a new life with a new husband. She felt as though her relationship with her daughter-in-law was over, but, Ruth "cleaved." And now, their relationship is in a totally different dimension. Naomi's heart has changed.

For the first time, Naomi uses a term of endearment never spoken to Ruth: *"my daughter."* The mindset of *"You better move back home,"* has drastically changed to *"Ruth, let me do something for you, baby! Let me be the mother you need me to be and help you find the right relationship so you're not working on that farm the rest of your life!"* Talk about a complete change of attitude! Hope has replaced hopelessness. Loneliness has given way to a sense of purpose and belonging. A life once wrecked is now seeing the dawning of a new day with the mindset of *"I can make it. There is someone in my corner and I'm not alone!"* Ruth's consistent life was now experiencing the ultimate victory: inspiring Naomi to dream again, believe again, and to once again engage in life!

A NEW REVELATION

Of all the remarkable things that had happened to Ruth, and now beginning to manifest in Naomi's life, this one piece of information was about to top it all! Full of new vision, hope, and revelation,

Naomi reveals Boaz's true identity:

> *"Now Boaz, whose young women you were with, is he not our relative?"*
>
> **Ruth 3:2a**

This man was more than just the person for whom Ruth has worked. More than the one who granted her favor. More than one of the most powerful men the region. He is one of Naomi's relatives. But, more than some distant third cousin, twice removed! He was their "kinsman."

Even though we do not use this word in our current vernacular, it carried major implications during this particular time of history. According to Leviticus Chapter 25, he held an extremely significant place in both of these ladies lives which carried specific obligations because of family relationships. For example, since he was the closest living male to Naomi and Ruth, it was his responsibility to rescue—or avenge—them from their bad situation. He was also a protector. If there was a violent crime committed against a family member, it was the kinsman's job to ensure justice was executed upon the person who committed the crime. Along with these, he was also a very significant link to their destiny.

He was their missing link!

THE MISSING PIECE

How frustrating it is to try and assemble something, only to realize a very important piece is missing? I experienced this trauma a few years ago when we bought our children one of those outdoor swing-set/fort/jungle-gym contraptions. At the beginning, I was really excited about doing this for our kids. (Okay, partly for them,... but it also guaranteed me the "Dad of the Year" award!) I could feel the Superdad "S" on my chest starting to pop out. But, what started out as a fairly simple project became more than I bargained for!

I called a couple of guys over to help and with our tool belts fastened and screwguns cocked and loaded, we thought, *"Just how hard can this be?"* After all, every one of us had construction experience, some earned college degrees, and we all were fairly intelligent. So, we cracked open the boxes and what did we see? About three million pieces of materials—screws, boards, supports, tarps, swings, ladders, etcetera. No problem. All we needed were the instructions and everything would fall right into place. After looking through the boxes, one of the guys found the instructions and begin to read them. There was only one problem.

They were written in French!

Here we were with all these pieces lying around but no directions that we could comprehend! This posed quite a problem. To make things worse, there were very few pictures to reference. All of us tried to remember anything from our high school or college French class, but to no avail. So, after about 20 man-hours of trial and error, we finally finished this *"How hard can it be?"* project. Oh, how much easier it would have been with the missing piece in tact.

How much easier would life be with the missing piece in place?

Ruth was about to find out.

THE REDEEMER

In Biblical times, there was also another type of relative called "the kinsman redeemer." It was the role Boaz would ultimately take. The word "redeemer" literally means "to buy back." During this time in history, it was not uncommon for someone to sell themselves into slavery to pay a debt. (The sad truth is, we still do this today! It's called Visa® and MasterCard®!) It was the kinsman redeemer's responsibility to pay off the debt and buy—redeem—them of slavery. If family members were forced to sell property to settle a debt, the kinsman redeemer would buy it back, keeping it within the family name. This practice was not without a cost. The new property owners would charge ten percent interest!

> You never know who God is going use to help redeem things back to you!

There was also another very important role of the kinsman redeemer, one that played a significant factor in Ruth's life. Because her husband had died prematurely, it was Boaz—the kinsman redeemer—who would take her as one of his wives and procreate with her. This would ensure the continuation of the family name and establish a legacy for generations to come. It also would be the missing piece to God's total restoration for Ruth and Naomi.

GUT CHECK

In studying this incredible story, something has always stood out to me. What if Ruth would have known that Boaz was, in fact, her kinsman redeemer? Would she have thought she had an "inside track?" Would she have seen it as her ticket out of hard labor? What if she would have completely relied on the fact that Boaz was responsible to take care of her? Would she have worked as hard? Been just as diligent? Displayed the same consistency of life? Of course, the more important questions would be these same ones—direct to you and me!

Here's a harsh reality: most of us would have taken the easy road and relied on who we knew, rather than how we conducted ourselves! Just think how easy it is to be consistent with the people we know can bless us? It's true! If we know someone has money or connections to help us get somewhere, it is easy to be reliable and be faithful with your relationship. We are friendly every time we see them! We even go out of our way to make sure they are recognized. If this person has a need, we are Johnny-on-the-spot and offer any assistance we can—with a smile! It's our human nature to show partiality for personal gain. And the Bible addresses it in James chapter two.

Partiality for the purpose of a personal agenda and making distinctions among people because of rank or influence is dishonorable before God. Actually, in chapter three, James writes that self-seeking envy is sensual and demonic. What we have to understand is this: we must be consistent with everybody. Why? Because you can never really tell where the blessing is going to come from. You just never know. I've learned this lesson the hard way!

There have been those who I just *knew* God had placed in my life to be my ticket to increase. They had all the right ingredients.

> Sometimes, people can look their best and be quite impressive, but ruin their opportunity by opening their mouth at the wrong time, to say the wrong thing.

Connections. Influence. Money. They just had to be God's answer for me! But in the end, they just flaked out. However, some of the people God has used for increase and blessing were those I completely underestimated. Lesson learned: I should never, ever underestimate the relationships in my life. One of the major voices in my life told me long ago, "*Trey, never forget that big doors swing on little hinges!*" You never know who God is going use to help redeem things back to you!

FROM MOTHER TO DAUGHTER

Naomi is on a roll! With a new vision and desire to help, she revealed that the person God would use for their complete restoration was right in front of Ruth's eyes. Now, another piece of "motherly advice" on how to approach Boaz and the events to come:

> "*He's winnowing barley tonight at the fleshing floor. Therefore wash yourself and anoint yourself, put on your best garment and go down to the threshing floor;* "
>
> **Ruth 3:2b**

It's the end of barley season, and Boaz is throwing a celebration party for everybody's hard work and dedication. (Sounds like something more employers should do in today's world!) Naomi was busy making sure her "daughter" was properly prepared for this moment. You can just hear her:

> "Now Ruth, baby, listen here. You need to be looking sly for this man tonight. Go down to the nail salon and get yourself a pedicure and manicure. And, girl, make sure they get all that dirt out from under your fingernails! Get some exfoliant and get all that dead skin off those knees and elbows. And don't forget your Estee Lauder® perfume!"

This was much needed advice and instruction to the young daughter who had never been exposed to such royalty. But, it was more than how she was supposed to look; the key was how to properly conduct herself.

> **"...but do not make yourself known to the man until he has finished eating and drinking. Then it shall be, when he lies down, that you shall notice the place where he lies; and you shall go in, uncover his feet, and lie down; and he will tell you what you should do."**
>
> **Ruth 3:3-4**

In other words, *"When you show up, don't walk in there being loud and obnoxious."* It is still great advice today, as well! Sometimes, people can look their best and be quite impressive, but ruin their opportunity by opening their mouth at the wrong time, to say the wrong thing. Oh, how they could use a "Naomi" in their lives!

ONE LAST INGREDIENT

All of the pieces are finally coming together. Ruth has shown herself faithful. Her kinsman redeemer has been revealed. Naomi's outlook on life has taken a complete change. Favor has been granted. The entrance to greatness has been opened and now, the way has been paved. Everything is in place. Restoration is in sight! But, it all hinges on one, remarkable aspect: Ruth's answer to the instructions given her.

> *"And she said to her, 'All that you say to me I will do.'"*
>
> **Ruth 3:5**

Again, Ruth's consistency shines through. At this point, she could have struck an attitude and said, *"Thanks for the advice, but I can take it from here. I got us here in the first place."* But, that would have been completely out of her character. She did what was expected: followed directions. No, "ifs," "ands," or "buts"!

And the next verse confirms this very thing:

> *"So she went down to the threshing floor and did according to all that her mother-in-law instructed her."*
>
> **Ruth 3:6**

Key words: *all that [she] instructed*! Not half. All! She would be every pastors' perfect member. Every boss's dream employee. Every teacher's perfect student. Whatever she would be, make no mistake; Ruth's character and life of consistency did not come easy! It required many, many personal sacrifices. But now, the results are coming forth—not just for her, by eventually for the sake of all mankind.

STARING OR WALKING

As with every aspect of this story, we need to, once again, analyze our own life and ask ourselves, "Who is being inspired by my consistency? Whose life is being positively affected as a direct result of my actions?" Even when we find ourselves in a difficult environment, what are we doing that is making a difference to those around us? Have we been constant even in the little things? Are we finishing what we said we would do and being people of our word?

> Even when we find ourselves in a difficult environment, what are we doing that is making a difference to those around us?

It really boils down to this question:

> "Are we staring at the entrance to our destiny, or walking through it, helping others along the way?"

That answer will define the next level of blessing a consistent life can expect to receive!

"Intimacy is being seen and known as the person you truly are."

—Amy Bloom

Chapter 8

BEHIND CLOSED DOORS

Consistency Brings Intimacy

Intimacy: the one thing everyone desires yet has the most difficult time finding. There are as many different definitions for intimacy as there are situations that need it. Husbands and wives know the key to any marriage is directly related to the intimacy they share. Children yearn for real intimacy with their parents. Even God is zealous for intimacy with us, His children. No matter which definition or scenario you use, one thing is for sure: intimacy requires emotional vulnerability, openness, courage, and trust.

I once heard a minister describe the vulnerability and courage required by intimacy as:

> "Running as fast as you can off the edge of the cliff, with no parachute and not knowing if there is anything to catch you before you hit the bottom."

Intimacy just doesn't happen! It takes preparation and planning. This is exactly what Naomi prepared Ruth for. Now, the question is, *"Will Ruth have the courage to give of herself and be vulnerable?"* Or, in other words, *"Is Ruth willing to take the leap of intimacy?"*

FOLLOWING THE PLAN

Naomi's instructions were specific, laden with purpose, and carried a much deeper meaning than what was seen on the surface. What she really told Ruth was, *"Go in there and take the position of a wife."* For women, in this time of history, to uncover a man's feet and lay across them was a vulnerable expression of her desire for intimacy. (Consider it Biblical, non-verbal communication!) It was not dirty or lewd. It was a customary expression of *"I'll give you my life, if you'll have me"* And Ruth followed her instructions to the tee.

> **"And after Boaz had eaten and drunk, and his heart was cheerful, he went to lie down at the end of the heap of grain; and she came softly, uncovered his feet, and lay down."**
>
> Ruth 3:7

She enters the room softly, never forcing herself in the door or making any demands. Remember, this is the same girl who had been working for this man in the field for the entire agricultural season; yet, she felt no shame in putting herself in a place of vulnerability. It brings up a very important point: if she would have not obeyed while in the field, it would have changed her relationship with Boaz. And, instead of the position of intimacy, it would have been one of apology. Before their relationship could have move forward, it would first have had to be repaired! But, that wasn't the case for Ruth.

...intimacy requires emotional vulnerability, openness, courage, and trust.

How important it is to be consistent, even when it doesn't seem to matter!

The truth is, we need to be more consistent with the people God has placed in or lives. We need fewer repairs and more opportunity to move forward. How awesome that Ruth could take her position as Boaz' wife with no relational baggage to overcome! Now, the responsibility was shifting...to Boaz. Just how faithful was this man, her kinsman redeemer, be toward her?

RIDE THE WAVE!

> *"Now it happened at midnight that the man was startled, and turned himself; and there, a woman was lying at his feet. And he said, 'Who are you?' So she answered, 'I am Ruth, your maidservant. Take your maidservant under your wing, for you are a close relative.'"*
>
> **Ruth 3:8-9**

Now, I don't know about you, but waking up to a woman I was not expecting, laying across my feet, would probably freak me out, too! Like Boaz, I would say something like, "*What in the world are you doing and who are you?*" That would be a little scary! Ruth was prepared for his reaction and not only told him who she was, but immediately asked for specific covering, and revealed his function in her life—her kinsman redeemer!

She confessed, "*I know who you are. I've come here tonight not because of who I am, but because of who you are.*" Still the foreign daughter-in-law of Naomi, she is asking Boaz to do the unthinkable: to protect her with his garment and bring her into his household. That's bold! Would her request fall upon deaf ears and go unanswered? Was she too vulnerable, too quickly? Did she make a request only someone with more clout should have made? Boaz quickly reinforced that she had done the perfect thing.

> "*Then he said, 'Blessed are you of the Lord, my daughter! For you have shown more kindness at the end than at the beginning, in that you did not go after young men, whether poor or rich. And now, my daughter, do not fear. I will do for you all that you request, for all the people of my town know that you are a virtuous woman.*"
>
> **Ruth 3:10-11**

That's a mouthful! And from a man who was, just a few seconds earlier dealing with the shock of a strange woman in his bed! And the impact of his answer is multi-faceted. Let's take a look.

- **HE BLESSED HER.** A man with Boaz's power had the authority to bless or to curse. And it was very significant. All throughout the Bible, great men of God pronounced blessing upon their offspring, their servants, and their people.

  The word "blessing" means "to have divine favor and to cause to prosper." Not only did he bless her, he also immediately recognized his role in her life by calling her "*daughter.*" Ruth was off to a good start—a Godly blessing from someone taking their rightful, responsible role in her life.

- **HE NOTED HER KINDNESS.** The word "kindness" literally means "covenant faithfulness and consistency." This was not a one-time event, where Ruth was faithful in something that would bring her recognition. Her *consistent lifestyle* was now being verbally recognized and honored.

- **HE RECOGNIZED A POWERFUL FORCE IN HER LIFE.** CEO's spend hundreds of thousands of dollars each year trying to create it. Sports teams live and die by it. And small businesses know it is one of the major keys to their success.

  This force is called *momentum*!

  From the first day Boaz recognized Ruth in his field, he was impressed. And the momentum started to roll! Even more extraordinary was the fact she displayed more kindness, more endurance, and more resiliency in the latter part of this whole process than in the beginning!

  This is what consistency does: it builds momentum so

you can finish stronger than you started. Ruth was on a roll and starting to ride the wave all the way to the top!

- **HE SAW HER INTEGRITY.** Boaz, being a little older than Ruth, had some insight into her character just by watching how she conducted her life. (Her reputation was speaking!) Think about how many willing and able young men worked with her in the field, every day. I'm sure she had no shortage of male opportunities. But, Ruth's mission was to find favor, not a husband! Thus, she wasn't swayed by money and kept true to the task set before her. And guess what? Someone noticed!

    And that someone was about to make all of her sacrifices worthwhile.

- **HE HONORED HER COMMITMENT.** How many times did Ruth want to give up, give in, take a short cut, or settle for the status quo? More than we can imagine. But now, all of her commitments were about to be honored with the words she had been waiting to hear: *"I will do whatever you want me to do for you!"*

    All of the temptations to quit were now in the rear-view mirror. Consistency is paying off!

OUR INTIMACY

Throughout this entire story, Boaz is the picture of God while Ruth represents us, the Body of Christ. All of Ruth's dedication and hard work was rewarded in one moment with her kinsman redeemer—

a moment of intimacy. A commitment of relationship. A dedication more than just a casual acquaintance. The same principle is true with us!

We must have an intimate relationship with our Heavenly Father, not a sporadic, need-based relationship that only looks to Him when we need help. Our desire needs to be much deeper. And, we are not the only ones who long for that type of intimate relationship.

> Real change is a product of our intimacy with God.

So does God!

How much does God desire a close, heartfelt, consistent relationship with His children? Enough to call us the "Bride of Christ!" Think about the one thing which unifies and strengthens the relationship between a husband and wife? Intimacy! Just like a husband, God is jealous over his bride, and our intimacy with Him creates a partnership of cooperation.

We learn His voice. We understand what He likes and doesn't like. We learn to love what He loves and hate what He hates. Like Ruth, as we vulnerably lay our lives at the feet of our Redeemer, His commitment to our relationship fleshes out. Then, through our constant love for Him and intimate bond, restoration is received.

I am a firm believer that God can supernaturally intervene and turn situations around in an instant. However, there is a principle displayed in the story of Ruth that we must understand: the majority of the way God desires to change our lives is through us!

both!) Not only that, he made sure that no one would see Ruth leave his room, thus protecting her from any rumors or malicious, personal attacks. This, my friend, is true integrity—and protecting it was a high priority!

HURRY UP AND WAIT

Just when you thought the motherly advice was finished, there was yet another round! And why not? It had proved to be right, so far!

> *"Then she (Naomi) said, 'Sit still, my daughter, until you know how the matter will turn out; for the man will not rest until he has concluded the matter this day."*
>
> **Ruth 3:18**

Doesn't she sound just like a mother? *"Set still." "Be patient." "Wait your turn."* Of course, when things start to turn around—especially if they have been difficult for a long, long time—we want everything right this instant! Our prayer turns from *"Oh, God, where are you?"* to *"Yes, Lord! Pour it all on me, now!"* It's a natural response, but not always the right one.

Throughout this entire journey, we have portrayed Ruth to be as close to the perfect person as humanly possible. But, she is human with the same emotions and frustrations that we all deal with. After hearing these newest words of advice, I would imagine her response (at least to herself) would be something like, *"What? Sit still? Are you kidding? This man has promised to do everything I ask of him. All we have to do is say the word, and it is ours!"* Again, she was being tested.

Another test of consistency!

Patience for her—or anyone, for that matter—is not an easy virtue or characteristic. Most people I know function better with a "to do" list of 20 items rather than the instructions to *"sit and wait."* We want to help the process along, add our two cents-worth, and arrive at our destination ASAP. Of course, to do this leaves out one very important element of our journey: faith! They Bible says when faith and patience work together, then we receive our promise. Patience is the component that forces us to rest in the promise that God is working on our behalf—even when it does not look like it!

Patience was working on Ruth's behalf. There was no need for her to become frazzled, deal with panic attacks and have a nervous breakdown. All she needed was the confidence that Boaz was going to take his responsibility and make sure they were restored to their rightful place. It sounds a whole lot like something Isaiah said:

"But those who wait on the Lord shall renew their strength; they shall mount up with wings like eagles, they shall run and not be weary, they shall walk and not faint."

Isaiah 40:31

From the outside looking in, it is easy for us to understand why Naomi was so persistent in protecting Ruth's rest. Why was it so important? Because the same field Ruth had labored in as a needy foreigner, *was about to be hers!* The same principle applies to our lives today.

MOVING OUT OF THE FIELDS

Maybe the field you have been working in is your marriage. You have labored and toiled for everything to work out right. Now, it is time to wait on God, use a little bit of faith, and watch it blossom into the marriage you have believed for. The same goes with starting a business. Maybe you have sowed in someone else's field, punched someone else's time clock, and gleaned from the corners. Your consistency and perseverance has now positioned you in the place of favor. You find yourself standing in the entrance of your destiny. Now what? Take Naomi's advice. Rest, and let God work out the details!

Being consistent in our place of patience is just as important as walking through the entire process. Our Promised Land is waiting behind our patience! Now, it is time to trust. Time to wait. Time to let God work on our behalf. This type of confidence—that God will take care of it all—only comes one way.

Through intimacy!

Just as in a marriage relationship, it is very hard to completely trust someone you barely even know. The more vulnerable and open we are in our relationship with God, the easier it is to sit back and let Him work it all out. Of course, our nature wants to "help Him out," but, He does not need our help. What He desires is our intimacy—the place where we can "run off the cliff without a parachute" (symbolically, of course) and have full confidence that God will be there! Our job is to stay consistent...

...even in the waiting!

Chapter 9

OUR KINSMAN REDEEMER

Consistency's Ultimate Promise

The previous eight chapters have shown how consistency can be applied to every aspect of our lives. However, there is one exception: redemption. Redemption is not earned through consistent works of any kind. Instead, it is a gift of God's unmerited favor, or grace. It is very important that we understand this important dynamic before seeing the conclusion of Ruth's life.

Even though she has done everything right and was now enjoying some of the benefits of her consistent life, Ruth's restoration lay completely in the hands of someone else. It was Boaz's sole responsibility for redeeming her and Naomi, *even if she had never exhibited such high character*. Redemption had nothing to do with her performance, it was Ruth's right.

REDEMPTION—GOD'S PLAN

We saw in Chapter 7 how redemption means to "buy back." A

deeper explanation would be to "avenge, deliver, purchase, and ransom." Redemption is the reflection of God's very nature. It started in Exodus Chapter 12, when God promised the children of Israel that He would rescue them from Egyptian bondage. The Bible says He would *"redeem them with mighty power."* It was the power of Passover.

For God's people to be redeemed, they had to follow very specific instructions: kill a spotless lamb, roast it, and eat the good meat, and then apply its blood on the exterior doorpost of their homes. This would mark them as God's chosen people. Then, when the Death Angel passed through the land, he would literally "pass over" any home marked with the lamb's blood. Through the act of bloodshed and submission, they were redeemed.

During the course of history, God began to empower certain people as agents of redemption. One was the kinsman redeemer (as shown in Chapter 7) who carried the responsibility for his family. He became their avenger; restoring land which had been stolen or undersold, redeeming those in slavery to pay a debt, and continuing the family name and heritage. Boaz carried this mandate for his family; but, more importantly, he was setting the stage our Kinsman Redeemer:

Jesus.

WILL THE REAL KINSMAN STEP FORWARD?

"Now Boaz went up to the gate and sat down there; and behold, the close relative of whom Boaz had spoken came by. So Boaz said, 'Come aside, friend, sit down here.' So he

came aside and sat down. And he took ten men of the elders of the city, and said, 'Sit down here.' So they sat down. Then he said to the close relative, 'Naomi, who has come back from the country of Moab, sold the piece of land which belonged to our brother Elimelech. And I thought to inform you, saying, 'Buy it back in the presence of the inhabitants and the elders of my people. If you will redeem it, redeem it; but if you will not redeem it, then tell me, that I may know; for there is no one but you to redeem it, and I am next after you.' And he said, 'I will redeem it.'"*

Ruth 4:1-4

Knowing the customs of the times, Boaz was looking for Naomi's closest relative—her kinsman—to have the first right of opportunity to redeem that which was lost. Of course, he marched right to the most populated public place—the city gate—to make his intentions known. He never went into some back room to cut a deal for Naomi and Ruth. No, he moved right to the place that was the "seat of authority" for the entire town. Now, everyone could hear and see, firsthand, what was about to happen.

As Naomi's kinsman relative approached, Boaz calls him over in the presence of 10 city elders. (It is called accountability!) He begins to tell him their story and then informs this gentleman of his right to redeem the land that Naomi and Elimelech had sold. It seemed simple enough, so the kinsman agrees. But, that was the easy part! The second matter at hand that was a bit more complicated.

Ruth's family lineage.

> *"Then Boaz said, 'On the day you buy the field from the hand of Naomi, you must also buy it from Ruth the Moabitess, the wife of the dead, to perpetuate the name of the dead through his inheritance.' And the close relative said, 'I cannot redeem it for myself, lest I ruin my own inheritance. You redeem my right of redemption for yourself, for I cannot redeem it.'"*
>
> **Ruth 4:5-8**

Now, the pressure is on! The kinsman's next responsibility was to marry Ruth. That did not seem so bad; but, they were also to have a son who would carry her deceased husband's name, Mahlon. Commitment was staring him straight in the face! And just like that, the kinsman became more concerned for his own future and declined all of his responsibilities.

Even though we do not know what caused this sudden change of heart, there are three things that could be good possibilities:

1. **TOO COMPLICATED.** Redemption, all of a sudden, became inconvenient. Perhaps his plans were to leave his inheritance for his own children. Adding another child would cloud the picture and muddy the waters. It meant more obligations and responsibilities. When redemption was easy—just gaining a track of land—everything was great. But, when a long term commitment surfaced as part of the package, the kinsman started backpedaling!

2. **TOO COSTLY.** Let's face it. Taking on a wife and a child is not free! It's not even cheap, especially when you already

have at least one wife and children! Perhaps the financial burden of buying a field *and* taking on a new wife all at the same time was more than he could bear. Either it was more than he could afford or more than he was willing to pay.

3. **TOO RISKY.** The risk factor was determined more by the *who* than the *what*. Buying land and marrying Ruth wasn't necessarily risky; it was his responsibility. But, to marry a cursed Moabite woman? That was risky. Maybe he was thinking about the potential cultural and racial challenges. Did he really want to introduce Ruth into his home? Was he willing to tackle all of the issues by having one of "those people" in his own household? Whatever the case, it was way too risky, and the first kinsman was not going to risk it.

The real kinsman was given the opportunity, but refused to accept it. But, it was okay. Actually, it was more than okay. It was God's plan in action! Now, Boaz has the full right to become the "kinsman redeemer." And, he took it.

> *"And Boaz said to the elders and all the people, 'You are witnesses this day that I have bought all that was Elimelech's, and all that was Chilion's and Mahlon's, from the hand of Naomi. Moreover, Ruth the Moabitess, the widow of Mahlon, I have acquired as my wife, to perpetuate the name of the dead through his inheritance, that the name of the dead may not be cut off from among his*

brethren and from his position at the gate. You are witnesses this day.'"

Ruth 4:9-10

Right in front of the elders in plain sight, he announces his intentions to redeem the land and to marry Ruth, perpetuating future generations of blessing. It sounds like such a perfect Hollywood storyline, doesn't it? But, it was much, much more than just a good story. Boaz was paving the way for another kinsman redeemer.

Jesus!

GOD'S PLAN REVEALED

The story of mankind mirrors the story of Ruth. Adam and Eve, like Naomi and Elimelech, once lived in a place full of God's Word and His presence, just like Bethlehem-Judah. However, Adam and Eve, through deception and one bad decision, fell into sin, thus enslaving all of humanity to sin and Satan. Our inheritance from our natural father, Adam, would now be poverty, disease, broken relationships, self-centeredness, condemnation, and separation from God.

But, God was not taken by surprise.

Isaiah 46:10 says God knows the end from the beginning. Before He ever uttered, *"Let there be light,"* He had already established a plan of redemption! Jesus Christ, the "Lamb slain from the foundation of the world," was God's chosen plan to redeem, or "buy back," a lost world. Many years passed after the Fall of Man in the Garden, and God's eternal plan finally came to this earth. Jesus emptied Himself of His divine attributes and came in the likeness and appearance as a man.

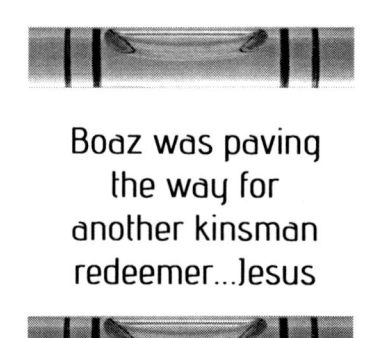

> Boaz was paving the way for another kinsman redeemer...Jesus

Friend, Jesus came to earth as our "Kinsman Redeemer!"

Just as Boaz, Jesus never hid His intentions of His mission on the earth. His business was in plain view of a city called Jerusalem. The difference was, our redemption could not be bought with money! The book of Isaiah says this:

"You sold yourselves (into sin) for nothing, and you shall be redeemed without money."

Isaiah 52:3

Actually, the price Jesus paid was far more valuable than all the money in the world...combined! It was the ultimate price—His own blood.

In front of an entire city, Jesus was stripped naked and beaten beyond recognition. His head, swollen twice the size of a normal human head. His back, ravaged by a beating so malicious, that bones were exposed. A crown of thorns was forced into his head, busting capillaries and sending burning, shooting pains throughout

His entire nervous system. Then, He was nailed to a cross and hung suspended between Heaven and earth for the entire world to see.

All alone, Jesus took the sin, shame, sickness, poverty, and emotional distress of all humanity. All of this torment for one reason: to be our "Kinsman Redeemer." What Adam had lost, Jesus "bought back" from Satan's domain, and destroyed the effects of sin on humanity once and for all.

DARE TO COMPARE

While Naomi and Ruth's closet kin rejected his responsibilities, Jesus never considered another option. Thank God our Redeemer never saw the same three reasons to remove Himself as the One to fully restore us back to God.

- **TOO COMPLICATED.** Jesus never allowed Himself to be inconvenienced by our need. Instead, He chose to bear all of our sin on the cross, becoming our representative. Because He fully accepted His responsibility, the defining power of sin, selfishness, poverty, disease, depression, offenses, perversions, and every other condition that holds humanity bound, has been destroyed! That was His mission—a mission He fulfilled.

- **TOO COSTLY.** God the Father gave what cost the most— His one and only Son. What does this say about us? That we are valuable in His eyes. Why would God send His best for someone He deemed to be worthless? He wouldn't,... and He didn't. Religion says you are not worthy, but that is a lie. You count to God. Your family counts to God. Your city is important to God. No price tag was too big. You were well worth His investment!

- **TOO RISKY.** Just think. Jesus knew all of our weaknesses and issues but never—not once—thought we were too much of a risk! That's amazing! He has done everything necessary to completely redeem us from bad experiences, failures, all set-backs in life. And guess what? Our baggage does not intimidate Him! In God's eyes, we were well worth all the risk.

PAY IT FORWARD

The most exciting thing about what Jesus did for us is how it affects the generations to come. Our Kinsman Redeemer died to put an end to all generational dysfunctions which have defined our lives for years. His mission to redeem and purchase all that was lost was accomplished so that a life of blessing, prosperity, and wholeness would not die, but live through our lineage.

> Jesus never died just so you could be a "good person" or experience religion.

When I think back over my life, I am so grateful that I have a Redeemer who ransomed and purchased my life! Now, I belong to God's family. He placed His name on my life and eliminated the effects of sin and Satan. Those blessings—and many others—will last throughout future generations. Thank God His blessings will now be in my lineage...unlike the generations which proceeded me.

My family history is littered with dysfunctions, damaging decisions, gross selfishness, and betrayal. Like many others, I know the sting of rejection by significant family members. Those feelings of abandonment and insecurity stimulated a great deal of internal struggles throughout my life. I am so glad that 2,000 years before I experienced any of that pain, Jesus Christ already paid the price for my healing, redemption, and freedom! While healing and redemption were instantly available, freedom came. Through acts of obedience like confession, forgiveness, honor, and submission to the Holy Spirit.

The day I totally abandoned my life to Jesus, I was free! Free of past mistakes. Free of dysfunctional family life. Free of emotional baggage. Free to live the life God had purchased for me to live. Now, through the blood of Jesus, the painful issues that once identified me will not have to define my children, or their children! God has healed my hurts, avenged every assignment hell had against my life, and replaced them with an ordained inheritance free from any family bondages.

I love my Kinsman Redeemer!

TWO DIFFERENT LIVES

If you are a believer in Jesus and are interested in having a life that is growing in every dimension, then this message of consistency is a vital key for your development. You must allow your character to be shaped in such a way to see your life completely restored, fulfilling the plan and purpose that God has ordained before creation. That God-ordained life is described as "more abundant," which means life over the top!

Jesus provided this life through His redeeming work of salvation. It is a free gift which was only dependant upon His death and resurrection. However, after receiving this free gift, you must begin to work out your salvation through His grace, allowing it to transform and change your life. The key for this transformation is a consistent life of dedication and covenant faithfulness to God. This type of committed life will allow you to see the plans and purposes of God begin to unfold right before your eyes. You will walk in your inheritance!

On the other hand, you may have never given your life to Christ. Maybe you are searching for answers to an unsatisfied, unfulfilled life. If this is you, it is important to understand that no amount of consistency, even in doing "good works," will earn your redemption. Jesus paid the price—in full—at the cross! He did it intentionally and on purpose.

And He did it just for you.

Now, you can exchange your life for His!

Jesus never died just so you could be a "good person" or experience religion. (Having the appearance of Godly morality, yet remain relationally cold toward Him). Neither was His death simply for you to escape hell. When Jesus died on the cross, He avenged all of the pain of your past and restored everything Satan has stolen from your life. It is called being "redeemed!" Friend, you have a Redeemer!

If you have never received this redemption into your life, then you are wasting what God has provided for you. Why not, right now, pray this prayer and start living the life Jesus purchased for you at the cross:

> *"Jesus, I believe You are the Son of God. I believe that You died for me and rose from the dead to give me life. I believe that You alone can redeem my life and make all things new. Right now, at this very moment, by faith, I give You my life. I want my life to totally belong to You. No longer do I want to live under the domain of Satan and sin. I confess that from this moment forward, I am a child of God, because I am redeemed. Fill me with Your Holy Spirit and grace me to grow in faith through my relationship with You. I do not belong to my past, I belong to my Redeemer, Jesus Christ! Amen."*

Jesus has now become your Kinsman Redeemer! It is time to begin your new, consistent, covenant life with Him! Remember the first thing Ruth requested when she found her kinsman redeemer, Boaz? She said this:

> *"...Take your maidservant under your wing,..."*

Ruth 3:9

She asked for covering and protection. In the same way, you now have the covering of the Almighty! Look to Jesus and say,

"Lord, put me under the wings of Your covenant. Cover me with Your grace. Cover me with Your kindness. Cover me with Your faithfulness." You can find your rest and your place *"under the shadow of His wing!"*

Welcome to your new life!

You will never regret this decision!

Chapter 10

ALL THE WORLD'S A STAGE

Fruit of a Consistent Life

What started out as a nightmare turned into a dream life. Ruth, a foreigner working in a field for handout, now owns the joint! The same can be true for anyone who sticks to their commitments and lives a consistent life with God and man. Even if you go to work some days and think, *"What am I doing here?"* just stay the course and be consistent. Who knows, one day you could end up running your entire division. Or better yet, become the CEO of the whole organization! This type of restoration and promotion is one of the fruits produced by a steadfast life.

Naomi, the distraught mother-in-law, is another perfect example. Just about three months earlier, she returned from Moab calling herself "bitter." She was angry at God, angry at man, and feeling completely forgotten and desolate. And now? God has sent her a redeemer to fight her battles, restore her land, regain her dignity, bring back the authority to her life, and ensure her inheritance she thought was lost forever.

Welcome to the dream life!

The abundant life!

ONE MAN, TWO FUNCTIONS

A redeeming, consistent God, plus someone who lives a consistent life, equals a supernatural breakout! If you don't believe it, just look at Ruth's life now:

> *"So Boaz took Ruth and she became his wife; and when he went in to her, the Lord gave her conception, and she bore a son. Then the women said to Naomi, 'Blessed be the Lord, who has not left you this day without a close relative; and may his name be famous in Israel! And may he be to you a restorer of life and a nourisher of your old age; for your daughter-in-law, who loves you, who is better to you than seven sons, has borne him.'"*
>
> **Ruth 4:13-15**

God's kinsman redeemer, Boaz, restored all that was lost in Ruth's life, including a son to continue her family name and legacy. But notice, he functioned in two separate roles: "restorer of life," and "nourisher." Even though these seem to be closely related, they are different in their meanings. Each serve a particular purpose and both are required for full restoration. Let's take a look at these two, distinctive functions displayed in Ruth and Naomi's kinsman redeemer.

THE RESTORER

A "restorer" is someone who gives back something which was lost to its original owner. This is exactly what Boaz did for Naomi—gave her another chance in life. Of course, Jesus, our Kinsman Redeemer, is our Great Restorer, but with one, added benefit: *things come back better than their previous condition!*

God's plan of restoration is not to make our lives the way they were before we encountered difficulty; it is for ultimate restoration. Bringing us back to the place where He originally saw us before the world was ever created! Ephesians says:

> *"Just as He (God) chose us to be in Him (Christ) before the foundation of the world...having predestined us to the adoption as sons by Jesus Christ to Himself."*
>
> **Ephesians 1:4-5**

What an awesome thought! Before God even started on creation, He saw you and me, picked us out, and determined that we would be His children! Before we were ever conceived in our mother's womb, we lived in the heart of God.

> *"For we are His workmanship (masterpiece) created in Christ Jesus for good works, which God prepared beforehand that we should walk in them."*
>
> **Ephesians 2:10**

When is the last time someone called you a "masterpiece"? Well, that's exactly how God sees you! Not some patched up, broken, old remnant of what used to be a work of art. No, you are His masterpiece! That's the real you God made you to be. The dysfunctional you is not the real you. The addicted you is not the real you. The depressed you is not the real you. The rejected you is not the real you. No matter how your life looks because of sin, Satan, or bad decisions, God is restoring you back to His original blueprint!

Just like Ruth and Naomi, even if your life is a nightmare, God is restoring you to dream life!

THE NOURISHER

To nourish something is to provide life-sustaining substance. A "nourisher" protects, defends, maintains, and supplies. To be nourished is different than being restored. Boaz's covenant was with both Ruth *and* Naomi! Not only was he bringing back everything that had been stolen or lost, but he was also ensuring they would not be put into those situations ever again.

Jesus played this same dual role when He visited the grave of His dear friend, Lazarus. After being dead for four days, Jesus comforted Lazarus' sister, Martha, by these words of hope:

"I am the resurrection and the life. He who believes in Me, though he may die, he shall live."

John 11:25 (NKJV)

What were the two things Jesus proclaimed to be? Resurrection and life." In other words, "restorer and nourisher!" Two separate functions. A few verses later, Jesus demonstrated His resurrection power by shouting, *"Lazarus, come forth!"* And he came out of the tomb, alive...*but with no life*. There was still some work to be done!

"And he who had died came out bound hand and foot with graveclothes, and his face was wrapped with a cloth. Jesus said to them, 'Loose him, and let him go.'"

John 11:44 (NKJV)

This is God's picture of abundant life! Someone who is restored from death to life *and then* nurtured and released into all God has called them to be. Aren't you glad that He does not stop with just restoration? God never goes half-way! Not only is He the Restorer, but He is the living, unending supply for our lives! Watch out! He might just use something that has been dried up for a long, long time.

Much like Naomi.

BROUGHT BACK TO LIFE

"Then Naomi took the child and laid him on her bosom, and became a nurse to him."

Ruth 4:16

Without being rude, crude, or risqué, do you see what the Bible says here? Who was nursing this child? Not mama Ruth; but *grandmamma,* Naomi! Physically, this does not make a whole lot of sense; however, we must see how powerful this is. This child began to receive life-sustaining nourishment from something that had dried up many, many years before. It must had been decades since Naomi's breasts had produced life-giving milk. But, because of God's covenant faithfulness and Ruth's willingness to consistently cooperate with His process, a dream for a future lived again.

> God has a plan is to restore every dead place in your life!

Friend, one of the most powerful benefits for a consistent life is it allows God to bring dead, dried up things back to life! Suddenly, Naomi was able to give life-giving nourishment to her dream. Suddenly, the loss of a husband and two sons in a foreign land had lost its sting. Suddenly, regrets were replaced by hope, and bitterness and dysfunction were washed away by God's healing water. Suddenly, Naomi had a greater reason to live!

What is God trying to use that you have considered dead? Maybe inconsistency has killed your dream. Your marriage and relationship with your children may seem un-repairable or dead. Maybe the ministry God birthed in you many years ago now lays buried underneath disappointment and failure. No matter what the circumstance, God has a plan to restore every dead place in your life! It is time to believe again. Time to dream again. Time to look forward to getting up in the morning and having a greater purpose than just trying to make it through another day. Dead things will live again and fuel your potential.

THE REST OF THE STORY

What a picture-perfect ending! Ruth is enjoying God's redemption. Naomi is living with a revived purpose, mission, and legacy. It is a remarkable testimony of God's faithfulness and the power of consistency. But, the story isn't quite finished!

> "Also the neighbor women gave him a name, saying, 'There is a son born to Naomi.' And they called his name Obed. He is the father of Jesse, the father of David."
>
> **Ruth 4:17**

On the onset, this verse looks like the normal pattern of life, their family's lineage. Ruth's son, Obed, grew up and had a son, Jesse. Jesse grew up and had a son, David. So, what is so important about Ruth's lineage? Well, for starters, it includes her great-grandson David. You know, the one who danced before the Lord, killed Goliath, and was the greatest king to lead the nation of Israel. But, it goes much farther than that!

Matthew chapter one explains a little bit about Boaz's history, as well. His mother, Rahab, was the prostitute who God spared when Jericho was destroyed! (Maybe this is why Boaz found mercy in his heart for Ruth, a foreign Moabite woman from a cursed and perverted people.) Generation after generation is recorded in this passage until Jacob becomes the father of Joseph. He married a girl named Mary, who gave birth to a son—Jesus! What does it all mean? All of humanity has been radically impacted because Boaz and Ruth fully cooperated with God's plan of restoration!

Aren't you glad they did?

The way for Jesus to come to this earth was paved by someone's dedicated and consistent lifestyle. Even with a history of tragedy and dysfunction, God's plan of redemption was at work! Think about it. One of Jesus' great-great-great grandmothers was a hooker! Another one birthed from incest! David, another in the lineage of Jesus, was a known murderer and adulterer. But, God was still at work! And, is still working on us today.

When we make the decision to surrender and enter into covenant faithfulness with God, our story changes—regardless of the past! Christ begins to be formed in us. Situations change. Restoration takes place. And then, it is released through us for future generations to enjoy!

YOUR LIFE, YOUR STAGE

During the entirety of this book, we have seen one of the greatest examples of consistency ever known to mankind. The principles are true, unchanged, and timeless.

Now, it's your turn! Time to make some adjustments. Time to live in God's best. Time to be consistent!

Making the decision to leave behind an inconsistent, wavering lifestyle is one of the best choices you will ever make. This type of life is very rewarding, but is never easy. The fruit of this life is fulfilling; however, there will be many obstacles and opportunities to retreat back into your old ways. Jesus talked about this internal battle with His disciples when He said:

> **"The spirit indeed is willing, but the flesh is weak."**
>
> **Mark 14:38 (NKJV)**

Any lifestyle change takes effort, time, and a conscience decision. I believe each person who earnestly desires to change can be changed! I am a testimony of how applying these principles can radically change your life, but I am not alone. Many others now enjoy the benefits of a life dedicated to consistency.

I believe you will be one of those who make that same decision and live the life God wants you to live. As you choose this new life,

Why wait to learn from your mistakes when you can learn from someone else's?

let me give you five areas that will set the stage for your new life... that life of consistency.

GET OFF THE WAAMBULANCE!

That's right! It's not a typo! The waambulance is a vehicle that carries whiners and complainers! All they do all day is *"Waa, waa, waa!"*

One day I was counseling an individual in my office. This person was complaining about everything. What they were going through. How badly they had been wronged. How they were down-in-the-dumps, etcetera. While listening to their rant, I was faced with two choices: to sit there and listen patiently or stop the waambulance and do something to help them. Needless to say, I chose the latter.

Right in the middle of our session I asked them, *"Do you really think you're the only hurting person in the world?"* The room became silent. Then I continued, *"I can name 10 people who have been hurt 10 times worse than you! Stop your complaining. All you are doing is complimenting Satan's plan for your life."* I wasn't being cold-hearted or mean, but I did get their attention! To sit there and be silent would have granted them permission to continue their pity party. But, I saw something better in them.

Sometimes, real solutions to problems are tough and uncomfortable. It is always easier to wallow in despair than to kick ourselves in the "blessed assurance" and own up to the circumstances which landed us in bad situations. The waambulance is a much easier ride!

For example, if you are not satisfied with your income, don't complain about it—do something about it. Don't get *bitter*—get *better*! Go back to school and finish your degree. Increase your learning, then apply what you have learned. Read books about successful people and learn their personal habits, the way they think, their pitfalls and mistakes. Why wait to learn from your mistakes when you can learn from someone else's? You can receive the benefit of the hard lesson without all the heartache! Believe me, anyone who seemingly has it "made in the shade" has had to endure many hot, dry days in the process.

Naomi would have ridden the waambulance straight to her grave, but Ruth said, *"Hey, we can't sit around and suck our thumbs until we die. If we throw a pity party, no one will come! We have to do something, and we have to do something now!"* And her commitment produced results!

COMMIT TO THE REAL PROCESS

It is so easy to look at successful people and think, *"Wow, I wish I could be successful like they are."* Well, what's stopping you? Most successful people—and I'm not only talking about what Hollywood perceives as successful—got to where they are by making good decisions and working hard. Professional athletes do not arrive at their skill level by only participating in their sport as a hobby. It takes intense training, strict diet regiments, long workout hours, and a strong, personal commitment to get their physical bodies into tip-top shape.

It is called: a process!

Every success in life is stimulated by a real, tried-and-true process. It moves you from where you are to where you want to be. Of course, there are always the counterfeit "short cuts" which are easier and require less work. But, the results fall way short of the real success the real process will produce.

A CRAZY CRAZE!

A great example of this is the video game craze, *Guitar Hero*™. This game allows people live out their musical fantasies by playing plastic guitars to famous rock songs. If they do well, the virtual crowd goes wild and the screen displays the words, *"You rock!"* For those not as "skilled," they are booed, and the screen flashes a real confidence booster: *"Loser!"* The game in itself is entertaining, but my question has always been, *"Why not spend the same amount of time and learn to play a real guitar?"* While others are living a fantasy playing Guitar Hero™, successful musicians are hammering out notes and chords on their instruments. Real instruments! And, hearing real applause, too!

The genuine process to life produces authentic results. Contrary to what some wish, God is not sending Tinkerbell to sprinkle magic pixie dust on your head and make it all better! Why settle for a "virtual" life with "virtual" benefits, when you can have the real thing? It all begins with submitting to the process.

KNOW WHO YOU ARE

You never, truly begin to live this "real life" until you discover your

God-given identity. Too often, people are defined by their family, peers, friends, or associates, and never see how God sees them. Learning this true sense of identity will allow you to live a focused, consistent life which goes beyond limitations. When you discover who you are in Christ and how He views you, you will never again settle for a counterfeit life.

Knowing your identity also helps to maintain your integrity when the heat is turned up and the pressure is on! When you live the "real life" God has provided, you will never lose your mind, your emotions, or your relationships. When you commit yourself to the real process of discovering who you are from God's perspective, it will be more beneficial than talent, education, or a well-formed network of relationships. It will, in fact, release you into a life beyond your imagination!

> ...if you want more than what you currently have, you must work for it—even in someone else's field!

DON'T BE AFRAID OF WORK

Even though you might not want to hear this, it is the truth, nonetheless. Work is not a bad, four-letter word! It is, however, a characteristic of consistent, successful people. Things just don't appear out-of-the-blue or show up by themselves. There is a tremendous amount of work and sacrifice involved.

Ever so often, I hear people say, *"Pastor Trey has got it made!"* One of the factors which have placed our family where we are today is two words: hard work! Finishing college, then seminary, and then working on a master's degree for three-and-a-half years while still working 40 hours a week, balancing a newly-married life, and starting a family was never easy! It required an enormous amount of dedication and hard work. In the end, we finished that season well.

But the work was just getting started.

Now, as the senior pastor of a growing church, I am on call seven days a week, 24-hours a day! So, even though I'm still not sure what it means to "have it made," I do know without the determination to work and stay with it—especially during the times I so badly wanted to quit—our family would not have the privilege of witnessing what God is doing today.

A TRUE TEST

While living out the process of dedication and hard work, I came to realize something very important: *sometimes working hard means serving someone else's vision and purpose.*

It is one of the toughest tests of consistency, but it is preparation for what God will eventually move you into. We all must be willing to lay down our own agendas, not serving our own "vision," and serve someone else.

Ruth had to! She worked hard in someone else's field to ensure the redemption of her and her mother-in-law. Ask yourself,

"Am I willing to work hard for someone even though I may not receive all the credit?" It is another true test of character.

Think about how Ruth must have felt. All of her hard work brought Naomi full recovery...and then some. (Naomi probably stayed home, watched Oprah, and complained the whole time!) Then, after Ruth had given birth to her new son, the neighbor women did not give her the time of day! *They sang their song of rejoicing to Naomi!* But, it was Ruth who worked the fields. Ruth who had the sore back. Ruth who nurtured blistered hands. Ruth even carried this baby for nine months and pushed him out. Yet, Naomi gets the party.

It doesn't seem quite fair, does it?

It sounds a lot like what Jesus said:

"If you have not been faithful in what is another man's, who will give you your own?"

Luke 6:12

There comes a time when you must be willing to lay down your "own thing" and make something happen for someone else. You must work just as hard for them as you would yourself, not expecting any of the credit or accolades. Just remember, God is watching and is faithful! What you make happen for others, God will make happen for you! The principle is simple: if you want more than what you currently have, you must work for it—even in someone else's field!

KNOW YOU HAVE A HELPER

Radical lifestyle changes are not easy and are practically impossible without the help of the Holy Spirit. Jesus describes one of Holy Spirit's functions as that of a "paraklete," or "helper." This type of "helper" was used by the Greeks during warfare. His job was to run alongside any soldiers who were struggling in battle and shout encouraging words to keep fighting. He would also warn them of any impeding danger. In essence, the "helper" became the eyes in the back of their heads, as well as the voice that produced courage if they began to grow weary.

If you are a Christian, the power you need to overcome the temptation to revert back to your old lifestyle is living right now *on the inside of you*! The Bible says you can do all things through Christ who strengthens you. (Philippians 4:13) Romans 8:11 says the same Spirit that raised Christ from the dead brings life to you! Jesus told His disciples in John 16:14-15 that everything the Father has belongs to Him, and everything He has He will give to the Holy Spirit to declare to you and me. That means the truth flowing within the Godhead is flowing to you and me as we listen to the voice of the Holy Spirit. How can we fail when we have such an advantage?

Even before you were a Christian, the Holy Spirit was with you. Now, as a Believer, He lives *in you* and desires to come *upon you*, making you stronger than you can ever be within your own strength. Avoid the temptation to retreat! Make a conscious decision to utilize His strength available to you. Believe God to help you the entire way!

LIVE FOR THE ULTIMATE GOAL

God's ultimate plan for Ruth—that Christ would be birthed through her lineage—was much more than she could comprehend. This would have been greatly compromised if she had given up and gone back to familiar Moab or had became offended. The entire time, there was something working that was bigger than her.

The good news is this: God wants to birth Christ through you and I today. His desire is for the world around us to see the glory of His Son. And how does that happen? Through a life that is consistent. A life that reflects God's covenant faithfulness. A life which never settles for the "status quo"—even at a young age!

If you are student in school, start now to be consistent in your school work! Don't settle for "C's" if God has given you the mind to make "B's" and "A's!" Begin to reach your maximum potential. Why? Because there is something greater happening than just good grades (even though it will make your parents happy, too!) God wants to birth Christ, through you! Not just on your campus, but one day at the law firm, the surgery center, on Wall Street, or in the military. How does this happen? Through a life which is dedicated to consistency and sold-out to pleasing Him.

Start now. The benefits are out-of-this-world!

YOUR TURN!

It is time! Time to get off the fence of indecision. Time to leave a life of inconsistency. Time to resist apathy, small mindedness, and lethargy! Just think of all the things God is waiting to do *in you* and *through you.* No longer will you just settle for what comes your way. This is the time to stand up and allow the Holy Spirit to ignite a fire of desire in you. If you are ready for this new life—the life of covenant faithfulness—that which has the power to change you and your future generations, then pray this prayer of dedication:

"Father, I thank You that You are the Consistent One. Your covenant faithfulness has been at work on my behalf even before I was conceived. You are my source of strength and life. You are the restorer of my soul and the redeemer of my life. Without You, my life is nothing. Thank You for the truth that I have learned. I am ready to apply this truth, and I ask for Your help. Holy Spirit, I realize that faithfulness is one of Your characteristics. Please rise up in my life and allow Your consistency to be lived out through me with my family, at work, at church, in my community, and especially in my relationship with You. Jesus, I want You to be formed in me and released through me. I must decrease so that You may increase. From this day forward, I will consistently follow after You. In Jesus name, Amen."

ENDNOTES

Chapter 1

1 Merriam-Webster's Online Dictionary. http://www.merriam-webster.com/dictionary/resolution.

2 Song of Solomon 2:15.

3 http://www.quotationspage.com/

4 http://www.divorcerate.org/

5 http://smallbiztrends.com/2008/04/startup-failure-rates.html and http://www.americanchronicle.com/articles/view/778

Chapter 5

1 http://www.kevinhogan.com/nonverbal-communication-body-language.htm

2 The actual acronym for "Yahoo" stands for "Yet Another Hierarchical Officious Oracle," named by founders, David Filo and Jerry Yang, Ph.D. Source: http://www.kevinhogan.com/nonverbal-communication-body-language.htm

CONTACT TREY JONES

TREY JONES

3944 Sardis Church Road

Macon, GA 31216

PHONE:

478.788.3621

E-MAIL:

lc@maconlife.org

ONLINE:

www.maconlife.org